CONTENTS

The King who has No Clothes 1
Glossary of Arabic Terms 134
Bibliography 145

This book is a work of fiction. Any resemblance between what is described and what you see is entirely coincidental. It is only a dream of a dreamer in the dream of Allah.

This book could not and would not have been written had it not been for the inspiration of Shaykh 'Abd al Qadir al Murabit. There is no power and no strength to do anything except from Allah.

Many thanks to all who have taught me, to those who taught me knowing they were doing so, and to those who taught me without knowing they were doing so. Al hamdulillahi wa shukrulillah.

Dajjal

The King who has no clothes

AHMAD THOMSON

Published by
TA-HA PUBLISHERS LTD.
1, Wynne Road
London SW9 0BD

Published by
Ta Ha Publishers Ltd.
1 Wynne Road
London SW9 0BB
England.

I.P.C.
P.O. Box 1143. Jos
Nigeria.

M.P.
P.O. Box 343
Brooklyn N.Y. 11217., U.S.A.

British Library Cataloguing in Publication Data
Thomson, A.
Dajjal:
1. Dajjal
I. Title
297' .22 BP166.89
ISBN 0-907461-50-6

Phototypeset by
Mayfair Typesetters, London WC2H 7ER

Printed in Great Britain by
Richard Clay Ltd, Bungay, Suffolk

And when the wizards came,
Moses said to them: Cast your cast.

And when they cast, Moses said:
That which you have brought is magic.
Surely Allah will make it vain.
Surely Allah does not uphold the
work of mischief makers.

And Allah will vindicate the Truth
by His words, however much the guilty
are averse.

QUR'AN : Sura Yunus
Ayats 80-82

بِسْمِ اللَّهِ الرَّحْمَنِ الرَّحِيمِ

In the name of Allah
The Merciful the Compassionate

In the country of the blind
The one eyed man is
King

DAJJAL

There are three aspects of Dajjal. There is Dajjal the individual. There is Dajjal as a world wide social and cultural phenomenon. There is Dajjal as an unseen force.

The word Dajjal does not appear in Qur'an. It appears in various collections of Hadith, including the two Sahih collections and the Mishkat al-Masabih and The Gardens of the Saliheen, in the sections which are concerned with the period of time immediately preceeding the end of the world. The prophet Muhammad, may the blessings and peace of Allah be on him, was sitting with a group of his companions one day during the late afternoon. The disc of the sun was just about to begin to disappear behind a wall. The prophet said that the time between their sitting there that afternoon and the end of the world, was as short as the distance between the disc of the sun and the top of the wall at that moment. This was fourteen hundred years ago.

Allah says in Qur'an that the person who is asked about the end of the world, that is the Hour, knows as much about it as the person who asks the question. Allah also says that mankind has only been given a little knowledge concerning the Hour. No one knows exactly when it will be, but Allah says in Qur'an that perhaps it is closer than you think. As far as you are concerned, the world ends for you when you die.

Many of the signs of the end of the world are clearly indicated in the Hadith collections, and whoever is awake and aware of the signs in the self and on the horizon, knows these signs and recognizes them when they appear. All the signs of the end of the world are now apparent, except for the last four major signs, and it would appear that even these are now imminent.

Amongst the signs already apparent are: that the poor and the destitute build tall buildings in which people glorify themselves; that the slave girl gives birth to her mistress, one meaning of which is that the mother who is enslaved by her work situation has children who grow up to be uncontrollable and who dominate and tyrannise the family situation; that women outnumber men; that there are many women who no longer give birth to children; that everyone is concerned with working so that not only the men but also the women go out to work; that there is an abundance of food, much of which has no blessing; that when a person is offered food it is refused; that time is short; that there are many people who are hard hearted and mean; that there is much fighting and killing of people; that there are women who wear their clothes like a second skin; that attempts are made to make the deserts green; that there are people who attempt to change the balance of nature and who interfere with and interrupt the basic cycles and processes of existence; and finally that the sun rises in the west, one meaning of which is that the life transaction of Islam is adopted by people living in the western world.

The last four major signs are the appearance of Dajjal the individual; the appearance of the Mahdi, the rightly guided leader of the Muslims who will fight Dajjal; the re-appearance of the prophet Jesus, on him be peace, who as well as breaking all the crosses, killing all the pigs, marrying and having children and praying with the Muslims, will also kill Dajjal; and the appearance of Juge wa ma Juge, a tribe of people who will scatter across the world, creating destruction.

It is clear that before Dajjal the individual appears on earth, there must already be present and established the system, and the people running that system, which and who will support and follow him when he does appear. Evidence of that system, and the people running that system, is evidence of Dajjal as a world wide social and cultural phenomenon, and Dajjal as an unseen force. The signs of these broader aspects of Dajjal, that is what Dajjal the individual will epitomise, are very apparent today, which would indicate that Dajjal the individual is soon to appear.

Amongst the descriptions of Dajjal in the Hadith collections we find the following: Dajjal has one eye, like a squashed grape. Dajjal can be heard all over the world at the same time. Dajjal will show you fire, but it will not burn you. Dajjal will show you water, but you will not be able to drink it. Dajjal will talk of the Garden, and make it seem like the Fire. Dajjal will talk of the Fire, and make it seem like the Garden.

2

These descriptions all fit the characteristics of today's media machines, and especially the manner in which they are largely used. Dajjal is also described in the Hadith as having many eyes on both sides, and travelling about the world in large hops. This description fits the characteristics of today's means of mass transport. Dajjal is described as having the letters KFR on the forehead. Some of the jets in the Israeli airforce have these letters painted on their noses.

The letters KFR are the basic root letters of the arabic word kufr, or kaffir. Kufr is to cover up and to reject. The kaffir is the one who covers up the true nature of existence, that is that there is no god only Allah, and who rejects the messengers who are sent by Allah to show people how to live in harmony with what is within them and with what is without them, and to worship and have knowledge of Allah. When the prophet Muhammad said that you should seek knowledge as far as China, he was talking about knowledge of Allah, or at the very least knowledge which leads to knowledge of Allah. If your knowledge does not come from fear of Allah, you have been deceived. Fear Allah, and Allah will give you knowledge. The kaffir rejects this. The kaffir is thus diametrically opposed to the mumin. The mumin is the muslim who openly affirms the true nature of existence, and who accepts and follows the example and teachings of the prophet Muhammad, may the blessings and peace of Allah be on him, the last of the prophets to have been sent by Allah before the end of the world.

It should be already clear that the kaffir system, and the kaffirs who control and believe in that system, are none other than Dajjal as a world wide social and cultural phenomenon and Dajjal as an unseen force. Dajjal the individual will be the epitome of the kaffir system, the ultimate kaffir, and therefore inevitably to be chosen as the leader of that system by the kaffirs who run that system, when he appears. The prophet Muhammad said that kufr is one system. The kaffir system is Dajjal. The three aspects of Dajjal are in fact interlinked and indivisible. Dajjal.

In the same way the Mahdi will be, when he appears, the epitome of Islam, the way of the prophet Muhammad, although it must be said immediately that he will be like a drop compared to the ocean of the prophet Muhammad, may the blessings and peace of Allah be on him. It follows that the Mahdi will be the one who is inevitably recognized and accepted by all true muslims as their leader. The prophet Muhammad said that the muslims are one body.

3

Kufr is at war with Islam. Islam is at war with Kufr. Dajjal will fight the Mahdi. The Mahdi will fight Dajjal. The prophet Jesus, who was not crucified, but taken by Allah out of this world into the Unseen, and another who looked like him crucified in his place, the prophet Jesus, on him be peace, having returned to this world, will kill Dajjal.

Dajjal has been the subject of much writing in the past. Prophecies relating to the Dajjal are to be found, for example, in the bible in the Book of Revelations by John, and in the writings of Nostrodamus. Many people have attempted to interpret these prophecies anew in the light of events taking place during their own particular lifetimes. Dajjal is usually referred to as the Antichrist in these prophecies and the commentaries on them. It is not known how reliable or accurate these prophecies or the commentaries on them are. It is quite probable that they came by way of the jinn.

The jinn are made of smokeless fire. They can see us. Only some of us can see them. We are made of water and clay. Angels are made of pure light. Angels are incapable of wrong action. They do not eat or sleep or procreate. They praise Allah continuously. They are the means by which the creational process operates. The jinn, like us, are capable of right action and wrong action. Some of them are muslim, some are kaffir, and some are munafiq, that is hypocrites who say they are muslim when in truth they are kaffir. The jinn often communicate with people, and from their knowledge of the unseen tell of events which lie in the future. Clearly, if the writings of John and Nostrodamus came by way of, or were influenced by, bad or mischievous jinn, then they are not entirely reliable, since, as is the case with many of the jinn who are the familiars of those who practice magic, or who communicate with mediums, for every truth that is told, several half truths and outright lies are also added. Given this element of possible uncertainty and error, the only way that the prophecies of John and Nostrodamus can be shown to be reliable is when what is said corresponds to what eventually happens.

As far as the written word is concerned, therefore, the Hadith contain the most reliable description of Dajjal and the events which are to take place before and after the appearance of Dajjal, wherever there is a reliable isnad, that is a reliable chain of transmission from the one who heard or saw what was actually said or done by the prophet Muhammad himself, to the ones who remembered what that person remembered by heart, to the one who recorded what they

4

remembered in writing. The Hadith which have been recorded in writing were only accepted after they had been scrupulously checked by the scholars who collected them, unlike the bible, much of whose contents is from unreliable sources and cannot be attributed to the prophets whose words and actions the bible purports to record. Allah says in Qur'an that the Jews and the Christians have changed and altered the original teaching of their respective prophets, and the numerous contradictions within the bible bear eloquent witness to this fact.

The prophet Muhammad did say however, may the blessings and peace of Allah be on him, that knowledge is the lost property of the mumin, who may pick it up wherever he or she finds it. The mumin is the muslim who not only believes in Allah, but also actually and actively trusts in Allah in the course of his or her everyday affairs. The muslim may believe in Allah whilst still relying on his or her own actions. The mumin relies on Allah for success. The muhsin is the muslim who knows that there is only Allah, and that accordingly reliance on other than Allah is an impossibility. The muslim, the mumin and the muhsin are all muslims, but they possess different degrees of knowledge of Allah. Those who fear Allah the most are the ones who have the greatest knowledge of Allah, because such fear only comes with such knowledge. The prophet Muhammad said that no other being feared Allah as much as he.

Knowledge comes to the one who purifies the heart by the grace of Allah. As the heart comes clear, the knowledge of the heart increases. This knowledge begins where the written word ends. For the ones whose heart is purified, so that the signs in the self and on the horizon, and they are the same, are recognizable and understood, the signs of Dajjal as a world wide social and cultural phenomenon and Dajjal as an unseen force are plain to see, and what is experienced is a confirmation and amplification of the information which the written word contains. The mumin is the muslim who trusts in Allah. Part of this trust is to trust others and to trust one's self and one's experience of life and one's interpretation of the signs in the self and on the horizon. This trust is complete when the person knows his or her self, for whoever knows their self knows their Lord, and whoever knows their Lord knows what comes from their Lord, which is creation, the universe and everything in it; and no form tangible or intangible, actual or conceptual, can be associated with Allah. Whoever has this trust and this knowledge is muhsin.

Reading is not the same as seeing. The seeing is a much stronger confirmation of what has been read. Books can only remind you of what has already been tasted and of what is yet to be tasted or what is capable of being tasted. It is the tasting which is important, not the record of the tasting, whether that record be audio or visual, on paper or on celluloid. To see is to know, but there are different seeings and different knowings.

Considering Dajjal as an unseen force, the presence of this force is indicated by the arrival of beings from another world who take possession of human beings in the same way as the jinn sometimes possess humans and animals. It may well be that Dajjal as an unseen force can, like the jinn, actually manifest as humans and animals without actually having to possess them, that is by taking on their likeness rather than by taking them over. It may well be that Dajjal as an unseen force is none other than a horde of kaffir jinn, as opposed to being beings of some other kind. It is not known from which world they come. It is known that there are many worlds. Allah is described in Qur'an in the Sura al Fatiha as Lord of the Worlds. Ibn al Arabi visited some of these worlds in vision, and describes these experiences in his book the Meccan Revelations. He names vast cities possessing technologies far superior to the one which some people on this earth boast of today.

The sign that this possession has taken place is that you see large numbers or groups of people all acting as one body, apparently possessing no individual identity. Although they look like human beings they simply do not behave like human beings, but more like robots. The large numbers of books and films which deal with this phenomenon are not mere figments of the imagination. They point to the reality of what has already occurred and continues to occur.

Since this aspect of Dajjal as an unseen force is in the Unseen, direct knowledge is only available to those who have been given access to the Unseen. Although the prophet Muhammad was given such access, he was not hungry for it. The desire for such knowledge is an obstacle to the one who desires direct knowledge of Allah. The evidence in the phenomenal world, that is the world which is apprehended by the senses, however, that this take over has taken and is taking place is to be found by observing the manner in which the social and cultural conditions in our world have changed, especially in this century, and by examining how life is conducted today. In other words, it is possible to ascertain the characteristics of Dajjal as an unseen force by

6

examining Dajjal as a world wide social and cultural phenomenon.

Considering Dajjal as a world wide social and cultural phenomenon, we see that the takeover is well under way, and that the time would appear to be soon approaching when it will be time for the Dajjal the individual to appear, simply because the systems and the people running those systems, that is the kaffir system, that is the Dajjal system, have apparently gained sufficient world wide control to be able to instate him as the leader they have all been waiting for, once he has been recognized and acclaimed as such.

Dramatic changes have taken place on the face of this earth in the last hundred years. The social groupings which used to be prevalent throughout the world, most of them based on the village pattern, a community of families who all knew and helped each other and which interacted with other village communities, have been rapidly eroded and depersonalized. In the large cities of today, the individual has become increasingly alienated from his or her self and from others and from knowledge of Allah, a cog in the consumer producer process who, when not at work or asleep, is often trapped in an infantile and unfulfilled search for illusory self gratification, which ensures that there is usually very little time left to reflect and consider where he or she is going, and no time to actually do something about breaking out of the recurring behaviour pattern in which he or she is trapped. Even where the social grouping of today is limited in size to the village number, the actual social transaction between its members is far less intimate and cohesive than in the past. There is less time to meet together and more time to watch television. There is less time spent working together and more time spent working alone. For those who have been born into this state of affairs, this change in social conditions is not always apparent. It is assumed that things have always been the way they are.

Perhaps the only way of appreciating how dramatic the change has been is to observe what happens when a multi national corporation decides to exploit the natural resources of a hitherto inaccessible region of the world. In a relatively brief period of time, the activities of the people controlling the corporation have not only disrupted the way of life of the people living in that area, but also eliminated their traditional sources of livelihood and thereby ensured that there is cheap labour available to carry out the work being generated by the corporation's activities. Suddenly everyone has a number and wants

7

this thing called money, and the social harmony which existed before the mine or the factory or the well or whatever became a reality, is gone. All this is done in the name of progress and civilizing the backward, but in reality the new lifestyle which is inevitably linked with the new technology, and with the mockery of real knowledge which the kaffir calls literacy and education, is the sign of the end of a human transaction in that area.

Another significant change in social activity, which is clearly linked with the degree of automation in any particular social grouping, is that whereas in the past a community used to be united by its worship of God, nowadays this basic and unifying element is often lacking in people's lives. In the western world this pattern of worship used to be predominantly that of the Christian religion, a peculiar amalgam of Paul's own ideas, Greek philosophy, the innovations of a priesthood, which itself was an innovation, in its attempts to compromise by all means with kaffir rulers, and finally a few traces of the original teaching of the prophet Jesus. Since this pattern of worship was not the same as that which was embodied by Jesus and his followers, it follows that it did not, and can not and never will, affirm the true nature of existence or lead to direct knowledge of Allah. It was and is inevitable that people would abandon this pattern of worship, the kaffir because he or she had no desire to worship Allah in the first place, and the true believer because he or she realized that the brand of Christianity which was being advertised had little to do with the original teaching of Jesus, and was not based on the behavioural pattern of him and his community, and would not lead to knowledge of Allah. It was the fragmentation of western society by the advent of the mechanised way of life, which made it easier for people to break free of the Christian pattern of worship. No worship was preferable to a pattern of worship which although performed in the name of Jesus did not conform to the pattern of worship which Jesus had in fact brought, and which has been long lost for ever.

It is interesting to note that there are some writers who have equated the Trinitarian Church, in all its different manifestations, with the Antichrist, since so many of its basic doctrines are not only invented by man but also openly contradict what Jesus himself taught, may the peace of Allah be on him, and since so many of its rituals derive from sources other than the lifestyle of Jesus and his community. This view is reinforced by the fact that it was the Trinitarian Church who in past centuries waged war on and eliminated all those Unitarian Christians, including the Nazarenes, the Ebionites, the Donatists, the Arians, the

Adoptionists, the Paulicians, the Illumnists, the Catharii and many of the Goths, who sought to follow the original teaching of Jesus and the way of life embodied by him. Once the last of these Unitarian Christians had been eliminated by the Mediaeval Inquisition and its successor the Spanish Inquisition, the Trinitarian Church then concentrated on attempting to eliminate all the unitarian followers of the prophet Muhammad, the Muslims, and despite its lack of success in this project continues in these attempts even today. The degree of success which was achieved by the Trinitarian Church in these attempts, both in the past and in the present, was, and is, only made possible by the fact that it worked hand in glove with the kaffir system, that is the Dajjal system, which of course was, and is, also committed to subverting and destroying the practice of a living and dynamic Islam.

In the light of this, it is clear that any apparent conflict between Science and Christianity is largely illusory and certainly only skin deep, since they both derive from the same system, that is the kaffir system, that is the Dajjal system. However it is equally clear that a distinction must be drawn between those Trinitarian Christians who are perfectly well aware that the way they follow is not the way of Jesus, and those people who in all sincerity wish to worship God and who have been misled into believing that the brand of Christianity which they follow is synonomous with what Jesus originally taught, and who up to now have had no chance of access to the living life transaction of Islam which is the prophetic lifestyle for this age, and which naturally bears a striking resemblance to the lifestyle once embodied by Jesus and his original followers, may Allah be pleased with them.

What has just been said about the Christians also applies to the Jews. Many of those who today call themselves Jews clearly do not follow the way of Moses, may the peace of Allah be on him, and indeed a great number of them do not even claim to be descended from the original Tribe of Israel for whom Moses was sent, but freely admit that they are descended from other forbears. Perhaps one of the most significant origins of these non jewish Jews is the people known as the Khazars, who were originally a small nation living in what is now Turkey and southern Russia. Their leader adopted the Jewish faith out of political expediency during the eighth century C.E. so as to avoid being conquered by the Christians who were approaching his kingdom from the north, or by the Muslims who were coming up from the south. He was perfectly well aware that this move would ensure a limited protection from those who also worshipped God. The descendants of the Khazars, noted for their expertise in business and financial transactions are now spread throughout the earth. The way of life which they follow is not the way of life which Moses and his community followed, may Allah be pleased with them. That way of life had already been lost when Jesus first appeared on earth. Jesus, it will be remembered, came to re-establish the way of Moses amongst the tribe of Israel and not to change it one jot or tittle. The fact that the scribes and pharisees, the self appointed priesthood of what had become the Jewish religion, did not even recognize who Jesus was shows how far astray they were from the original way of Moses even then, and that was twenty centuries ago. Sometimes described as the thirteenth tribe of Israel, the descendants of the Khazars are equated by some as being synonomous with one of the last four major signs of the end of the world, that is the appearance of Juge wa ma Juge, since they are in reality Jews but not Jews. If this be true, then we see that they are intimately linked with the appearance of Dajjal, since many of them today are in high positions of control in the various interlinking systems which together make up the kaffir system, that is the Dajjal system.

There are those who are only too eager to point out that what has been said about the Christians and the Jews also applies to the Muslims, and that there are many people who call themselves Muslims who are not following the way of the prophet Muhammad and his community. This is quite true, and it is partially a measure of the success enjoyed by the Christians and the Jews in their attempts to subvert and destroy those who have sought or who seek to follow the way of Muhammad and his community, may Allah be pleased with them.

One of the chief methods used by the kaffir system, that is the Dajjal system to erase living Islam is to introduce the kaffir way of life into the muslim countries, whilst disguising this fact by describing it in islamic terminology. Nearly all the traditional muslim lands are today controlled and governed according to the precepts of the kaffir system, and not according to what is in Qur'an. Although the prophet Muhammad said that some Muslims would follow the example of their predecessors, meaning the Christians and the Jews, faster than a lizard makes for its hole, he also said that not all of his community would go astray. There are still many Muslims who today follow the same pattern of life as that which was followed by the prophet Muhammad and the first Muslim community which formed around him. The point is, that although there are people who say they are Muslims but who do

10

not follow the way of Muhammad, at least the way of Muhammad is still available for those who do wish to follow it, and at least there are people who still do follow it.

The main difference between the Jews, the Christians and the Muslims is that the Jews do not know or do the prayer which Moses did, the Christians do not know or do the prayer which Jesus did, and the Muslims do know and do the prayer which Muhammad did.

The way of Moses and the way of Jesus have been lost. The religions of Judaism and Christianity have been manufactured and introduced in their stead. These religions are an integral part of the kaffir system, that is the Dajjal system. The Dajjal system is the complete antithesis of the prophetic way of life, as embodied not only by Moses, Jesus and Muhammad, but also by all the prophets as far back as Adam, may the peace of Allah be on all one hundred and twenty four thousand of them.

There are three basic patterns of social grouping in the world. There is the simple community which lives in fitra, that is in simple harmony with existence but without following the prophetic pattern of worship of Allah. There is the Muslim community which as well as living in harmony with existence also worships Allah in the manner indicated by Allah through the prophet Muhammad. Finally there is the Kaffir society which neither lives in harmony with existence nor worships Allah consciously.

In Reality of course every single atom is in its place and the overall harmony of existence eloquently proclaims the majesty and beauty of the Bringer into Existence and the Bringer out of Existence and the Only Existent, Allah.

We have seen how the pattern of life followed by the small community living in fitra and by the muslim community has been considerably eroded and destroyed, especially in the last century, by the spread of the kaffir system, that is the Dajjal system. In order to appreciate the characteristics of this system, which is outwardly the expression of Dajjal as a world wide social and cultural phenomenon and inwardly the manifestation of Dajjal as an unseen force, it is necessary to examine it in greater detail.

The way in which today's kaffir state is managed and controlled is by means of a highly centralized government. The advance of technology, especially in the realms of communication and travel, together with the use of complex computerized information storage and retrieval systems, has made widespread control from one place a reality. Most kaffir states are police states. Compared with the situation a hundred years ago, the degree of surveillance and control exercized by the rulers over the ruled is staggering. Much of this control is made possible by the form which work takes in today's industrial society. It is significant that the most common form of business concern today is the large corporation, whether privately or state owned, which often not only has branches all over any one particular kaffir state, but also all over the world. Everyone who works within a particular corporation structure is controlled by the manner in which that corporation operates. People are obliged to put the rules of the corporation above the application of common sense and humanity in the conduct of their everyday lives. Even the individual concern or the small business is highly regulated in what it may or may not do. Everyone is always told that these rules are for their own good, but they are never given the chance to see what life would be like without them.

It comes as no surprise to find that those who control the government of a kaffir state usually control the large corporations too. The elite of the kaffir controllers control the kaffir legal system, which is used to control all the other interlinking sub systems in the kaffir system, that is the Dajjal system, by determining what form they may take and what the people who work within them may or must not do. This means that life in a kaffir state is highly institutionalised, standardised and regularised. The most common social grouping today is centered around the work nexus. It is pyrammidical in form. The manner of its control is pharaonic. This enables the few to enslave and control the many, often without the many realising just how great the degree of control being exercised over them is. All kaffir institutions are run as a business concern, whether it be the legal system, the government system, the factory system, the university system, the hospital system or the media system, to name but a few.

All these institutions are geared to enable the effective running of the producer consumer process, which is today's predominant kaffir religion, enthralling the many with its myriad rules and controlled by its priesthood of kaffir experts. The consumer producer process is promoted as the ideal way of life by all those who at present control the kaffir states of the so called modern world. This is not surprising, since it is they who benefit most from that process and gather most of its financial rewards.

When establishing the consumer producer process in what is called the third world or the under developed countries, the colonisers, as has already been noted, have always disrupted the way of life which was being followed by the indigenous population prior to the colonisers' arrival. The basic approach has always been to persuade people to produce more than they need. To do this they have to be persuaded to work longer hours than before, and the women have to be persuaded that they will be free if they go and work in the factory all day. In order to make the work an attractive proposition, the people are offered money, but only enough to ensure that once they are dependant on it they will have to keep on working to have it, because they have not earned enough to save up. In order to make the money seem worth anything, the people are persuaded to want products which they never wanted before and many of which they simply do not need. Once you have the people wanting the products, they have to obtain the money to buy the products, which means they have to work to obtain the money. Thus in a very short period of time a large number of people can be persuaded to abandon their former way of life, in order to manufacture the products which they have been persuaded they want, and so get paid to buy them.

Naturally there are those who, although they have been persuaded to want the goods and the money to buy them, either cannot obtain work or cannot be bothered to obtain work. Instead they turn to crime. This provides the ideal excuse for the kaffir controllers to introduce their legal system to protect those who are working and at the same time increase their control over the working population. This also means the creation of more jobs for those who are needed to make the kaffir legal system work, including not only the bureaucrats and office staff but also the people who have to build the offices to house them, and the courts and prisons to deal with the people who will not play the consumer producer game. Naturally the fines collected in the courts do not provide a sufficiently large income to pay for all these buildings to be erected and to supply the people working in them with a decent salary. Accordingly additional taxes have to be levied. This necessitates more office space and creates more jobs for the tax collectors. It means people have to work harder to maintain their spending capacity. It means people try to avoid paying the taxes, which means the people in the legal system are given more work. As the taxes are increased and as the accepted value of money diminishes, because prices are put up to gather additional income without having to do any additional work, the work force becomes disgruntled. It attempts to organise and alter the status quo. As a result more laws are passed to control their activities. This means more work for the people in the legal system. In no time at all the consumer producer process has been firmly established. The working population is enmeshed in a bureaucratic system of organized anarchy, in which their attention has been concentrated on their daily bread. As the activity within the consumer producer kaffir state becomes more complexified and diverse, there inevitably comes the stage which we are now witnessing in those countries in which the kaffir consumer producer process can be said to have originated: Total Collapse.

It is this cycle of self destructive activity, the kaffir consumer producer process, which has all but destroyed the radical alternative to this behavioural pattern, the prophetic lifestyle. Millions of people are trapped in the kaffir system, that is the Dajjal system today, and although many of them are not happy with it, it seems unlikely that they will be able to appreciate what living Islam is until the collapse of the consumer producer process in the west is further advanced than at present, so well have they been programmed to believe that a life based on consuming and producing is civilised, whilst a life based on the way of Muhammad is primitive.

The consumer producer process ensures that people are treated like children, encouraged to work hard and enjoy their play, ,and not to ask awkward questions. The ignorance of the people who control that process and of the people who are controlled by them is displayed by the fact that they are unaware of the true nature of existence, and of what happens to you after you die. They take existence for granted, pretend that they are not going to die in the foreseeable future, and think that when they do eventually die, they will simply become dust.

Those who follow the prophetic life pattern, which is based on a revealed message from Allah and not on the speculation and experimentation of the kaffir so called "expert," know that everything comes from Allah and returns to Allah. They know that they are on a journey from Allah to Allah. They know what happens after death: the questioning in the grave, the period of waiting until the end of the world, the being brought back to life on the Last Day, the Balance being set up, the weighing of one's actions and intentions, the decision being made as to whether you are for the Fire or the Garden, and finally your going to one or the other. Those who follow the prophetic life pattern not only know what lies on the other side of death, they also appreciate how short life is, and they act accordingly. Clearly for the one whose sights are fixed on the Garden, or only on Allah, the exploitation of others in order to build up wealth and power in this life, is clearly a worthless and pointless proposition. It is only an attractive proposition to the kaffir because he or she thinks that this life is all there is, and accordingly attempts to reconstruct the Garden in this life and in this phenomenal world.

The prophetic life pattern is grounded in worship of Allah. The five prayers which the Muslim does each day are sometimes referred to as the five pillars of the day. They support your day and keep things in perspective. Of course it is necessary to work, for it is only in the Garden that food comes to you whenever you want it, but the mumin is not subservient to his or her work situation, only to Allah. It is much more difficult for a mumin to be anxious about his or her provision, because he or she knows that Allah is the Provider, and that whoever remembers Allah is remembered by Allah, and that whoever praises Allah is fed by Allah.

Muslim economics is based on the voluntary sharing of wealth by the rich with the poor. What the kaffir state seeks to achieve by means of heavy taxation enforced by repressive measures, the muslim community achieves by voluntary sharing. Voluntary sharing is only possible where the true nature of existence is known. The one who has been given wealth knows firstly that it is from Allah, secondly that if he or she shares it as he or she has been commanded by Allah this will help take him or her to the Garden, and thirdly that if he or she does not share it then such greed may take him or her to the Fire. The one who wishes to see the face of Allah also knows that he or she must give out of what Allah has given him or her. The prophet Muhammad said to Abu Dharr in the shadow of the Kaaba one day that those who were in most danger of going to the Fire were the very rich unless they spent in every direction. He also said that giving out is a shield from the Fire. The reason why a muslim community has no need of a police force, or of prisons, or of a repressive legal system, is that the prospect of the Fire provides a far greater deterrent to committing antisocial or selfish actions, and the prospect of the Garden provides a far greater incentive to do right and generous actions, than the deterrents and incentives needed in a kaffir state by people who think that the Fire and the Garden are imaginary places dreamed up by the Christians in the past so that corrupt priests could blackmail simple people into parting with their wealth.

The truth is that although the heaven and hell conceived of by the Christians, who no longer have access to the original teaching of Jesus, may not bear any actual resemblance to the Fire and Garden, and although corrupt Christians in the past have used the threat of their hell and the promise of their heaven to make money out of people who feared God, nevertheless the Fire and Garden are real and you will be going to one or the other. It should be quite clear to anyone who reads the descriptions of the Fire and the Garden in Qur'an that no one in their right mind would have invented the life after this one in order to make this life more bearable, since the possibility of going to the Fire is a horrifying one, and no one can be certain which of these two abodes will be his or her destination in the next life.

Giving out forms the basis of Muslim economics and of increasing wealth, since whatever you give in the name of Allah, Allah gives you back at least ten times as much. The kaffir attempts to make money out of nothing by charging interest, and when the interest rates go too high there comes a time when the kaffir currency is seen to be what it is, absolutely worthless. The muslim gives out and leaves the rest up to Allah. The kaffir has to be ruthless to become a millionaire, whilst the muslim has to be generous to achieve the same object. Whereas the mark of a kaffir state is vast taxation and the accumulation of capital, the mark of a muslim community is minimal taxation supplemented by voluntary giving out and with no accumulation of capital. The prophet Muhammad once said that if he was given a mountain of gold the size of mount Uhud, he would be ashamed if it had not been disposed of within three days. The kaffir state attempts to systematize and orchestrate distribution of wealth, to the annoyance of all except its ruling elite who benefit from the manner in which that distribution operates, whilst in a muslim community the distribution of wealth takes place naturally and unexpectedly, to the delight of all who trust in Allah.

The people in a muslim community find their meaning in worship of Allah. Allah says in Qur'an, "I did not create man or jinn except to glorify me." Allah also said on the lips of the prophet Muhammad, "I was a hidden treasure and I wished to make myself known, so I created the Universe." The knower, the known and the knowledge are one. The people who are trapped in the kaffir system, that is the Dajjal system, do not know this. They have been conditioned to find their meaning in the consumer producer process and to accept the system which enslaves them.

It has already been stated that the kaffir system, that is the Dajjal system, is formed of interlinking systems. In order to understand how the interlink operates, it is necessary to look at some of the more influential systems more closely. It must be remembered that it is the systems and structures which are being examined, and not necessarily the people in them.

Whereas some people work in order to live, many now live in order to work. The kaffir factory system is an inhuman and degrading system. It treats people as a necessary, yet expendable, part of the consumer producer process. Increased automation means that the people who man the machines are increasingly subservient to the machines. They are obliged to keep pace with the machines. In a factory which produces twenty four hours every day, the people have to be highly regulated in order to ensure that the machines do not have to be stopped and the flow of production obstructed. The only way to survive in this environment is either to act like a robot, or to be one.

Success in the kaffir factory system is measured by the degree of control which you exercise over others, and by the degree of control which is not exercised over you, and by the amount of money which you make in the process. The more products you can afford, the more successful you are. The more you embody the illusory ideal of the perfect consumer producer as depicted in the media, and there is more than one ideal in order to have as many profitable markets as possible, the greater is your reputation in the consumer producer game.

People are educated in order to work, not in order to understand themselves or the nature of existence. The kaffir educational establishments are themselves like factories, only the end product is not merely a product, but a person who will help to make products either directly by working in the factories, or indirectly by managing the factories or by working in one of the interlinking sub systems which ensure that the final product can be successfully advertised, distributed, sold and consumed. Whether an individual is prepared to work in the public sector, the private sector, or the services sector, the kaffir educational system ensures that he or she has been programmed to look at the world largely in terms of the cost of living, the number of unemployed and the gross national product. The kaffir media system maintains this economic perspective in conjunction with the kaffir educational system.

The only way to keep people enslaved in the consumer producer system is to keep them in ignorance. Accordingly they are given selected information during their so called education and by the media, and not real knowledge. They are conditioned to desire the bits of paper and the know how which will give them the best of positions possible in the producer consumer hierarchy. If the conditioning is not successful, it is almost inevitable that the kaffir legal system will be called into play in order to implant the basic ideal of the consumer producer process more vigorously upon the person in question. The individual who has a good work record and a job waiting for him or her is usually dealt with more leniently in the kaffir courts of so called justice. Some people are so impervious to the kaffir educational conditioning process that they end up spending a great deal of their lives in prison. The result is the same, an individual who has been rendered ineffective by means of institutionalisation.

The great majority of people who teach in the kaffir educational system do not have real knowledge, that is knowledge of the Real, that is Allah, or they would not allow themselves to be part of that system and accordingly part of the kaffir producer consumer process which, as we have already seen, only appears to be an attractive proposition when Allah and the Last Day and the Fire and the Garden are firmly forgotten. Furthermore real knowledge is free. As soon as a fee is charged, you can be sure you will only be receiving information for your money, most of it useless. Useful information is defined as that information which leads to real knowledge. The opposite of that is useless information.

Those who have real knowledge, and share it, do not charge money for it, because they know that it is not their knowledge to sell, and because they know that their knowledge is a gift from Allah which has only been given to them because they wanted it and Allah wanted it, not because they could pay for it. The only kind of payment which is necessary to acquire real knowledge is worship of Allah and fear of Allah and having a good expectation of Allah. Ultimately it is only given by the grace of Allah if that is what Allah wants. You will not acquire this knowledge by seeking it, but only if you seek it will you acquire it. Allah says in Qur'an, "Fear Me and I will give you knowledge," and "Remember Me and I will remember you," and "Ask and I will answer." Allah is the Rich, and not in need of what appears to be other than Him. All that appears to be other than Him is in need of Allah. Allah is the Knowing and the Knower of every separate thing that befalls us, the All pervading. Allah gives knowledge to whom He pleases, and His outpouring is vast. The kaffir producer consumer system is designed to stop you from finding out.

The kaffir university system as we know it today, the apex of the kaffir educational conditioning system, is big business. It not only completes the conditioning process for those who are to be given control of the consumer producer process and the systems which regulate and define its functions and make its existence possible, but also ensures that a handsome profit is made whilst so doing. It also ensures that the future controllers of those countries which have been successfully colonised by the originators of the consumer producer process can be suitably programmed to uphold that process and protect the colonisers' interests, long after these countries have been granted so called independence and apparent release from the control of their former kaffir coloniser masters. This conjuring trick, whereby the colonisers appear to relinquish control whilst in reality still retaining it, is sometimes called neo colonialism.

Fifty years ago there were hardly any universities. Those which did exist had a relatively small number of students whose primary objective was knowledge, although admittedly these universities did cater primarily for the offspring of the then ruling elite who were educated in order to take over control as and when their relatives died. As the new universities began to materialise, they at first retained the character and aims of the older universities, or at least tried to imitate them. Within ten years of the end of the second kaffir world war, a marked change in policy had become apparent. Whereas in the past the acquisition of knowledge, which is always a hopeless proposition anyway in any institution whose teachers have no access to a living and intact prophetic guidance, had been the main consideration, now two fresh objectives emerged. The first objective was to expand as quickly as possible so as to have as many fee paying students as possible, despite the fact that this would mean that a close and meaningful relationship between the teacher and the taught would no longer be possible. The second objective was to channel more people into what are called the sciences, and to lay less emphasis on what are called the arts. Of course these objectives were dressed up in suitable terms such as, everyone has a right to a decent education, and, in the interests of national safety and livelihood research must go on. In reality the so called education was far from decent, whilst the very methodology used by these kaffir educational institutions often ensured that what was being searched for would not be found. Useless research is encouraged in the kaffir university because it keeps people busy and provides the fortunate few with an opportunity to build up a reputation and a sizeable income out of nothing.

What lay behind this change in policy which clearly emerged after the end of the second kaffir world war was this: A power struggle was taking place behind the scenes between the Christian church and the people who were laying the foundations of the consumer producer process as we know it today. The scientific movement had found out enough about the nature of existence for anyone with intellect to realise that the Christian metaphysic, whose basis was the untenable doctrine of trinity which had never been mentioned by Jesus and which had not been completely formulated until about five hundred years after he had left the earth, was no more than a fairy tale and no less than a lie. It is interesting to note in this context that what little knowledge the kaffir scientists have acquired through their method of research is confirmed by what is in Qur'an, which is after all the A to Z of existence as revealed by the Originator of all that which appears to exist.

The primary struggle, however, in this power struggle between the Christians and the scientists, was not between those who claimed to know the nature of existence. It was between those who wanted power over the land and the people living on it. The real purpose behind the new policy was to ensure the uniform conditioning of as many people as possible. It was important that there was only one version of the meaning of life available for public consumption. The fact that the Christian version could be scientifically disproved meant that the scientific version gained more acceptance. Although many people still believed in God, they did not have the means at their disposal, that is a living and intact prophetic guidance, to integrate that belief with the scientific facts with which they were being presented. Thus although the scientific version was clearly not the whole truth, it could not on the face of it be disputed, and in the meantime the magical word, research, could be invoked to show not only that what was not yet known was being discovered, but also that research was accordingly necessary to make these discoveries. It was on this basis, that the scientists could answer all the questions which the Christians could no longer avoid by telling people that is a mystery or that is not important as long as you have faith, that the scientific version of existence, plagued as it is with speculation and theory, came to be widely accepted in the western world. Whereas the Christians know that God exists, but cannot explain the nature of existence, the scientists have some inkling of the nature of existence but cannot relate it to God.

Once the scientific version of the nature of existence and the scientific approach to existence had become widely accepted, the people who championed this version and this approach, inevitably gained control of the kaffir educational system. The research which they in fact encouraged was orientated largely towards the development of the producer consumer system. This development depended on there being a uniform conditioning of as many people as possible. Only as a result of effective and widespread conditioning could overall control of the general population be ensured. It was necessary to imbue the people with the notion that the meaning of life was to be found in producing and consuming. As the numbers of students increased, dramatically after the second kaffir world war, the people who taught at and controlled the kaffir universities changed. The old school either retired or died, and those who replaced them were either dedicated to the producer consumer process and its ideals, or else unaware of what that process was, and where its development was leading.

The few who were aware of the change of approach to life which was being engineered by means of the kaffir so called educational system, and who objected to it, could not afford to object too strenuously or to attempt to change the trend as long as they wished to retain their position, and its accompanying reputation and salary, in the kaffir educational hierarchy. There was nothing they could do to change the system from within that system, and even less if they left it. The interlinking systems which together form the kaffir system, that is the Dajjal system, supported the kaffir educational system too effectively for anyone to be able to change it merely by opposing it. Severing a head or two from the many headed beast does not kill the beast. Indeed those who control the kaffir system, that is the Dajjal system, encourage a certain amount of dissent since it is easier to rule a people when they are divided against each other, and also those who are not easily placated by minor cosmetic changes to the system, which do not in fact disturb the status quo, usually end up exhausted and ineffective if they try to change the system single handed. If too many people try to change the system together, and look like succeeding, they can usually be dealt with by means of the kaffir legal system. All that is needed is a law making their group illegal, and then anyone who persists ends up in jail.

As the numbers of students at the kaffir universities increased, it became necessary to provide the buildings in which to house and teach them. The erection of these buildings, or the acquisition of buildings already standing, provided a good source of income for many people, and of course helped to establish the producer consumer process more firmly in the process. As the kaffir university industry expanded it took on the usual characteristics which typify the kaffir institution. Gradually the kaffir university system, together with the sub stratum of polytechnics and colleges which had grown up below it, became increasingly impersonal and meaningless until it had become what it is today, just another production line in the kaffir system, that is the Dajjal system. The relationship between the teacher and the taught was such, and the academic environment in which that relationship functioned was such, that transmission of real knowledge, even if the teachers had had it in the first place, was an impossibility. The numbers were such and the systems were such that the only transaction which could take place was the systematic and impersonal provision of vast quantities of structured information, much of which was and is utterly useless. The better a parrot a person was, the more clever he or she was considered. Wisdom was reduced to a word with a devalued meaning. The takeover, not only as far as the kaffir university system was concerned but also the rest of the kaffir educational system which prepared people for that university system, was completed, and continues to function today.

Students at today's kaffir universities are encouraged to indulge in university politics and thereby to play a non influential part in the running of the university, to work and to play so that they can let off steam whilst still submitting to their conditioning, and finally to seek promising jobs in the consumer producer process once they have been duly awarded their bits of paper which are commonly called degrees. The majority of students do not even know that they are being conditioned, or what the nature of their conditioning is. The few who do realise what is going on either nevertheless choose to go along with it, or else they drop out. Of those who drop out a few can overcome the inertia to wake up and look beyond the kaffir conditioning process for real knowledge. Indeed it is one of the characteristics of the kaffir system that is the Dajjal system that whilst you are in it, that is whilst the state of mind which its conditioning process induces, whether by education or media, continues to prevail, it is virtually impossible to conceive of any alternative to it. The world view, that is the version of the meaning of life, which is engendered and nurtured by the kaffir educational and media systems is Kufr. Only the one who is not content with this view and who has rejected the kaffir system that is the

Dajjal system, is in a position to appreciate what Islam is and to begin to follow the way of the prophet Muhammad, may the blessings and peace of Allah be on him.

The kaffir hospital system has in the last fifty years become an integral and important part of the producer consumer process. It exists to keep people in working fit condition. Many of the illnesses which it has to deal with are the direct result of the way in which people live, and are obliged to live, by virtue of the way in which the consumer producer process operates. The kaffir system, that is the Dajjal system, creates its own illnesses, thereby creating work for those who are employed in the kaffir hospital system. The kaffir hospital system is run as a business. Everyone is paid for what they do. The livelihood of a large number of people depends on other people being ill, and the way of life, which has evolved as an inevitable result of the way in which the modern kaffir producer consumer state is run, ensures that there are more than enough ill people to keep the kaffir hospital system in business, thereby ensuring countless others, who supply the hospitals and doctors with the tools and medicines of their trade, steady and profitable employment.

The capacity of the kaffir system to create unnecessary jobs and meaningless activity in any sphere of life is something almost to be marvelled at. This is in marked contrast to the situation to be found in the simple village community living in fitra or in a balanced muslim community. Of course there is illness in these communities, for illness is the manifestation of imbalance and everyone loses balance at some time or other, but firstly the healthy not only look after the sick, but also know how to look after the sick, and secondly they do not make a business out of it. Since these two kinds of communities do live in harmony with existence, since they know what to eat and what not to eat, and since they have a balanced way of life, it inevitably follows that there is far less illness around than in a kaffir society simply because there is far less imbalance. If the heart is at peace, it follows that there will be no illness which is caused by nervous strain, anxiety or tension. If the correct food is eaten then the illnesses which originate from the stomach, and most illnesses do, will not arise. Life is very simple.

The prophet Muhammad was once sent some costly medicines from Egypt. He returned them with the message that his way of life was its own medicine, and the best of medicines. He was so finely balanced that his only major illnesses arose when people tried to poison him whether by means of food or magic. The prophet Muhammad, may the blessings and peace of Allah be on him, said that if the heart was well then the whole body would be well, and if the heart was ill then the body would be ill. The heart is the centre of one's being. It is the means by which we know the self and Allah, and whoever knows their self knows Allah. All the outward actions which together give the pattern of life embodied by the prophet Muhammad have an inward and beneficial effect on the heart. The heart is not at peace unless you worship Allah. Only by the remembrance of Allah is the heart made serene. The only way to worship and remember Allah in every single lived moment is by following the way of Muhammad.

Like the kaffir factory and educational systems, the kaffir hospital system is run like a production line. As automation has increased, it has become correspondingly more depersonalised. Medical staff are obliged, by the sheer number of people with whom they have to deal, not to become involved with their patients. It is easier to treat them as objects than as humans. Since most of the people who run the hospital system have usually been university conditioned, it usually follows that the vast majority of them have no real medical knowledge. Many of their so called cures are only skin deep. In the same way that the university professors toy with ideas in their theoretical speculations, so the doctors experiment with drugs in their medication. More often than not the patient is a human guinea pig, the final test for a new drug once no more can be learnt from trying it out on other animals. Their best medicine is the loving care of the nursing staff.

The kaffir doctor is obliged to experiment, because he or she does not understand the nature of existence. Many kaffir doctors today are even unaware of the basic knowledge, which is so important in the practice of medicine, that all matter is composed of varying combinations of the four elements, that is air, fire, earth and water; that these elements are respectively hot wet, hot dry, cold dry and cold wet; that the body of a human contains four humours that is blood, black bile, yellow bile and phlegm; that these humours are respectively hot wet, hot dry, cold dry and cold wet; that all foods have their own medicinal properties and, depending on the elements from which they are formed, are hot, dry, cold or wet in varying degrees and combinations. Illness occurs in the body when there is an imbalance of the humours. This imbalance can be corrected by taking the food which has the opposite qualities of whatever qualities the illness has, whilst at the same time refraining from the food which has the same qualities as the illness. The kaffir doctor denies this, saying it is

24

primitive. Homeopathy, which is a complementary way of medicine to the way just described in that it treats like with like rather than with opposite, is usually treated with the same disdain by the kaffir practitioner. Similarly the ancient methods which are used to free the subtle energy flows in the body, such as acupunture, are treated with suspicion. In reality the kaffir doctors' opinions as regards these enlightened ways of treating illness only mirror the reflection of their own ignorance in the matter.

It is interesting to note that in order to ensure that the kaffir medical view of treating illness predominates, the kaffir legal system makes it illegal to practise as a doctor unless you have the appropriate kaffir medical qualifications and initials after your name. This approach is typical of the kaffir system, that is the Dajjal system, as a whole. Any view or course of action which contradicts the kaffir norm is rendered ineffective and of minimal influence, by making it illegal before the stage is reached where it might become effective. Once an action or approach to existence has been deemed to be against the law, then the weight of the whole kaffir legal system can be used to squash it. In effect the kaffir system, that is the Dajjal system, ensures that if you disagree with it, you may criticise it but you may not actively try to change it.

As far as surgery is concerned, many of the operations carried out in the kaffir hospitals are unnecessary, and many of the operations which do appear necessary are needed to deal with ailments which are directly caused by the way in which people live in a kaffir society. If the patients had had a balanced way of life in the first place, they would not have incurred the illness which caused them to arrive in the operating theatre. Once in the operating theatre, again many patients are no more than guinea pigs. Let us see what this will do to him. One of the descriptions of Dajjal in the Hadith states that Dajjal will cut a man in two, so that it seems that he is dead, and then put him together again, so that it seems that he is alive and well. This description aptly fits what goes on in many a kaffir surgery, as well as covering some of the psychological disorders, such as schizophrenia, which inevitably result from the kaffir way of life. The good surgeons do, however, perform many invaluable operations.

The ignorance displayed by the manner in which the kaffir medical profession treats physiological disease is only equalled by the lack of knowledge which is evident in the way in which they attempt to deal with psychological disorders. Since they do not know the nature of existence, it follows that they do not know the nature of the human self. It follows that they do not know how to treat the ailments of the self. They have no unitary knowledge. They do not know how the universe and what it contains comes into being, nor how it goes out of being, nor how it appears to be in each moment between its birth and death. Since they have a fixed, as opposed to a dynamic, view of reality it follows that they have a fixed idea of what normal is, and anyone who does not fit that idea is considered abnormal, and accordingly is assaulted either physically or psychically in an attempt to bring them within the bounds of that definition. Since at the very best they only have a partial idea as to how the human self works, they are reduced to the barbaric practice of rendering the brain quiescent and ineffective, either by drugs and heavy sedation, or electric shock treatment, or lobotomy. The fact that they concentrate on the mind, that is on the contents of the head, in itself shows that they have completely missed the point, since it is the heart which requires attention. Recitation of Qur'an is enough to still the heart and calm the mind, thereby rendering the kaffir psychologist's approaches obsolete. The reason why many people in today's kaffir societies suffer varying degrees and kinds of madness is because they try and figure out the nature of existence with their heads, when only the heart is capable of arriving at such an understanding. Some liken the heart to the sun, and the head to the moon. The moon does not generate its own light. What light it has is reflected light from the sun. Once the heart has been illuminated by the rememberance of Allah, the intellect is then illuminated, and not before.

Perhaps the greatest error of the kaffir psychologist is to give reality to the illusory self, that is the self which does not really exist. They say we are what we think we are, or what we think others think we are. To the people of real knowledge this illusory self does not exist. It only appears to exist if an imagined reality is given to it, since what ever you imagine, is real for you. If you cease to imagine anything, existence does not cease, but rather you see existence as it really is. You see, wherever you turn, the Existent. Wherever you look, there is the face of Allah. There is no reality only Reality. In effect the illusory self is nothing more than a solidification of events obscuring a light which is the true self, the light of Allah. The kaffir doctor gives reality to that solidification of events and not to the light which it obscures. That is why he or she is kaffir: his or her action covers over the truth of the matter. By giving reality to what is unreal and by refusing to give reality to the Real, Allah, it follows that the kaffir psychologist is not going to have any success in the cures which he or she attempts to perpetrate, since whatever he or she does will almost inevitably be without reference to the true nature of existence and will accordingly be out of harmony. The so called cure of the kaffir psychologist is imbalance piled on imbalance, darkness piled on darkness.

The mumin doctor, and by this term we do not mean a muslim who has been subjected to the kaffir educational conditioning process in the field of medicine and who has accepted that conditioning, the real mumin doctor knows that the illusory self has to be dismantled before the true self emerges. This is achieved by purification of the heart, the centre of your being. This purification is achieved by the rememberance of Allah. The transformation of the heart only occurs by the grace of Allah. This purification and this transformation of the heart in the inward can only take place if there is a corresponding purification and transformation in the outward, that is in your existential behaviour pattern.

The only way of life which today makes this inward and outward purification a possibility, and for the one who follows it a reality, is the way of Muhammad. This is the means by which, once the heart has been purified, one knows one's self and one's Lord, and these two knowings are the same knowing. In Reality the knower, the known and the knowledge are one. To gain this knowledge, it is necessary to stop thinking altogether, which means that the one who has this knowledge cannot be trapped by the kaffir educational and media conditioning processes, since this kaffir conditioning is only successful where the thought process has been attracted, harnessed and then programmed. There is no deep reality to the kaffir psychologists' definitions of what normal is. They are arbitrary definitions. Deep sanity is to affirm the reality of Allah, and this affirmation finds its fullest expression in the one who follows the prophetic life style. This life style finds its fullest expression in the way of the prophet Muhammad, may the blessings and peace of Allah be on him, the first and last of the prophets in the prophetic cycle. His way is its own proof. The one who follows it benefits from a healthy body and a peaceful heart and the tranquillity which comes with real knowledge.

The ignorance of the leaders of the kaffir medical profession today is evidenced by the fact that they do not have the cures for the physiological and psychological ills which are the natural result of the consumer producer process, and the lifestyle which comes with it. They concentrate more on the ailments once they have manifested, than on the original cause of their having manifested in the first place. From one view point life is like a chemical equation: Given certain ingredients and certain conditions, the result which follows is inevitable. If you follow the kaffir lifestyle you will be in turmoil, and are for the Fire. If you follow the way of the prophets you will be at peace, and are for the Garden. The Qur'an is the only book on the face of the earth today which contains all the equations. It is the A to Z of existence, and in it is a guidance which shows you what to do in every situation. The prophet Muhammad said that in Qur'an is a medicine, so take what you need from it.

The one who has no Qur'an in his or her heart is like a ruined building, is like a dead person already in their tomb. Since the kaffir doctors do not have access to Qur'an, and indeed would refuse it if it were offered to them, they proceed on a basis of trial and error which they describe as a path of evolution and progress. They may discover some of what is in Qur'an by accident, and indeed much of what forms the basis of kaffir medicine today was originally culled from muslims in the past, who only received their knowledge by Allah and by following what is in Qur'an, but the kaffir doctors can only have a limited knowledge of what is in Qur'an because they do not follow what is in Qur'an themselves. They have no unified field of knowledge. You can only understand what is in Qur'an by embodying what is in Qur'an.

As with the kaffir factory and educational systems, the kaffir medical system is not really concerned with healing and with what is beneficial, but with money. It is big business, creating business for the vast pharmaceutical concerns which provide its drugs and equipment, and keeping thousands upon thousands of people usefully employed in patching up people, so that they too can be usefully employed. It is more common to hear the medical students of today talking about the large fees they hope to earn once they have passed the right exams and collected the right bits of paper, than the number of people whom they hope to heal, or more importantly the means by which that healing is to take place. The kaffir medical system is an integral part of the kaffir consumer producer process. It promises great rewards for the fully qualified. It plays a very important role in the overall management of the kaffir system, that is the Dajjal system. Closely linked with the kaffir educational system and the kaffir legal system, its leaders wield great influence in the kaffir state. A hundred years ago the kaffir medical system as we know it today did not exist. During that relatively short period the takeover has been completed.

The system which makes the operation of the kaffir factory,

educational and medical systems a viable proposition, and indeed which controls the operation of all systems in the kaffir system, that is the Dajjal system, is the kaffir legal system. The kaffir legal system makes the interlink of all the other kaffir sub systems possible. It is thus the heart of the kaffir system, that is the Dajjal system, as a whole. The kaffir legal system defines the structure of all other systems in the kaffir state, regulating what they may do and what they may not do, and ensures that any alternatives to the kaffir system, that is the Dajjal system, are rendered ineffective by either making them illegal, or at least by severely restricting them. The kaffir legal system also dictates what human behaviour is permissible in the kaffir state, thereby ensuring the effective control of the majority of people within that state. Anyone who actively opposes the kaffir legal system finds him or her self locked up in prison in a very short space of time. In effect the kaffir legal system is utilised to ensure that the consumer producer process runs as smoothly as possible.

The inevitable resultof such a state of affairs is the police state, that is a society divided against itself, where one half feeds off the other half. The kaffir police force is given wide powers and freedom of action. Basically its membrs can do in the name of the law what for anyone else is against the law. They are paid a lot of money to do this, even though the taxpayers who provide the money and who are tyrannised by the police do not want either to pay the taxes or to have the police force. The argument used is that if there were no police force there would be chaos. The answer to this is that there would be chaos amongst those who are kaffir, but not amongst those who are muslim. The way of Islam means that those who follow it do not need a police force, because each individual is his or her own police man or woman. Instead of policing others the muslim looks to his or her own actions in the knowledge that he or she is answerable to Allah for them. Furthermore the nature of the muslim community is such that the roots and causes of crime which flourish in a kaffir society simply do not have a place to grow in the muslim community. As in the field of kaffir medicine, so in the field of kaffir laws, many of the ills and ailments which provide the legal system with work are the direct results of the way in which the kaffir system, that is the Dajjal system operates, and of the lifestyle which the people working in that system are conditioned to follow. The kaffir system, that is the Dajjal system, creates needless activity patterns in order to keep people occupied, and in order to make money out of that activity. Of course some of the police are helpful, but then helpful people always are.

After the kaffir medical system, or rather in conjunction with it, the experts of the kaffir legal system are required to undergo the most rigorous of kaffir conditioning educational processes, before they are permitted to operate. In effect this is a screening process, whereby those who are inimicable to the kaffir system, that is the Dajjal system, are prevented from finding out too much about its workings and are weeded out. As in the kaffir educational system and the kaffir medical system, it is clear that there has also been a change in personnel as it were in the kaffir legal system. This is evidenced especially by the fact that although God is mentioned from time to time in accordance with legal tradition, many of the people who exercise control in the kaffir judicial system clearly do not fear Allah or even believe in Allah. If they did, they would act very differently to the way they do at the moment. Indeed the manner in which a typical kaffir trial is conducted is a pale imitation of the Last Day. The person who acts as judge and decides what is to be done to the person in the dock acts on many an occasion as if he or she were God, often completely oblivious of the fact that there will come a time when he or she will stand alone before Allah, answerable for all that he or she has done.

By examining the changes in the legal system over the last hundred years it is clear that the take over has taken and continues to take place. Whereas a hundred years ago the laws of most of today's kaffir states were based on the remnants of the teachings of Jesus, peace be on him, and on common sense, today they are unashamedly designed to control and manipulate wherever possible. It is said that the laws have been passed to create a more just society, but in reality their effect has been to keep the majority of people firmly enmeshed in the producer consumer process. Again that insidious doctrine, the kaffir doctrine of evolution, is invoked in order to persuade people that the kaffir legal system is progressing and getting better, which it will continue to do until it finally collapses, brought down by its own weight. Like the kaffir medical experts, the kaffir legal experts do not understand the nature of reality. They give reality to what has no reality and refuse to give reality to the Real, Allah. It follows that they do not know how to deal with reality. All their attempts at social engineering are grounded in speculation and arbitrary theories. They have no certainty. It follows that the alleged objectives of the kaffir laws will never in fact be realised. Thus for example the development of the kaffir laws designed to uphold human rights has been paralleled by a vast increase in the degradation and ill treatment of humans throughout the world, much of that ill treatment and degradation being caused by the infliction of laws formulated by the very same kaffir legal systems which invented human rights law. In reality these human rights laws are given publicity in order to persuade people that they have a just legal system, but not in order to actually establish a just society.

The only cure for the social fragmentation which is today everywhere in evidence, and which is being aided by the way in which the kaffir legal system operates even though that system is meant to be curing that fragmentation, is Islam.

One of the results of kaffir colonisation has been that the kaffir system that is the Dajjal system, and especially its kaffir legal system, has been successfully implanted in nearly all the countries which, before the coming of the colonisers, were ruled in accordance with what is in Qur'an. This means that at the time of writing this, there is not one country in the world which is free from the kaffir system, that is the Dajjal system. The study, however, of history from a Qur'anic perspective and not from the currently favourite kaffir perspective, clearly demonstrates that any community, country, or group of countries, has always flourished when following prophetic guidance, and always suffered when its people abandoned that guidance. The Qur'anic study of history also clearly shows that the people in any one country, during the passage of time, fluctuate between kufr and iman. There is a time when the majority of them are kaffir, and there is a time when the majority of them are mumin, and there are times of transition between these two opposites. This pattern of activity is in accordance with the true nature of existence, which is the manifestation and dynamic interplay of opposites originating from one source, Allah. Since everything lies in its opposite, and since the majority of people in the western world have not been following a prophetic guidance for several centuries, it follows that the advent of Islam in the west is not only the cure for the sick kaffir states of the west, but also absolutely inevitable. Allah says in Qur'an that there is no changing the way of Allah.

In the last fifty years we have witnessed a dramatic increase in the number of new laws which have been formulated, as well as the multitude of regulations which are drawn up under, and by virtue of, the so called authority conferred by these laws. Never before in the history of mankind have humans been so regulated in what they may do and what they may not do. People are punished for the least deviation from the legally defined norm, even in circumstances where neither person nor property has been injured or damaged. The doctrine of strict liability means that a person can be found guilty of an

31

offence even where there is no blame, and even if, in the circumstances of that case, he or she was doing what according to common sense was most appropriate. The more laws there are in a country the more offenders there will be. The more offenders there are, the more business there is for the people who operate the legal system, and the richer they become. Even in situations where injury or damage to person or property does occur, and even if the person who caused the damage or injury has made good that damage or injury, he or she will still be subjected to the kaffir legal process and punished. This indicates that the kaffir law is not used to maintain balance, but has become an idol which if violated must be swift in retribution. The kaffir legal system is not used to maintain social harmony, but to maintain social inequality by means of oppression and repression. It favours the people who control the kaffir system, that is the Dajjal system, and is used by them to control and manipulate the people who are enslaved by that system.

Many of the kaffir laws in force today arise out of a situation and a society in which there is no trust between people. In a time when many people have become hard hearted and mean, they seek to take advantage of others rather than to help them. Such people are described in Qur'an as the mutafifeen, that is the defrauders, who demand full measure from others but give short measure in return. Laws are passed to curtail their actions, but as quickly as the laws are passed the defrauders find ways to evade them, which means that more laws have to be passed to stop up the loopholes as they become apparent. Since it is often the defrauders who make the laws in the first place, it comes as no surprise to find that there are always some loopholes left open permanently for the lucky few who know about them. As well as this ever growing multitude of laws, life is further complicated by the doctrine of judicial precedent which states that all past judicial decisions are binding on judges when deciding a case which has a similar fact situation. Since no situation is ever exactly repeated again in creation, and since all judicial decisions are made subject to the personal prejudices of the judges who make them, it inevitably follows that judges are obliged to reach decisions which are patently unjust because of a case which may have been decided many years ago, when life and attitudes were very different to what they are today. The only way around the doctrine is to indulge in word play and intellectual dishonesty, which ultimately causes confusion and uncertainty when a decision arrived at by those means has to be applied to another similar fact situation later on. The result of all these laws and all these regulations and all the past decisions which have been reached, often when the law then was very different to what it is now, is a complex web of do's and don't's which is for ever changing or being changed, so that only the kaffir legal expert who spends his whole life in this maze has any idea of its geography. Indeed the maze is now so large that the need to specialize in one particular area has become a necessity, until the time is reached, if it is ever reached, when all the information is stored on magnetic tapes and we have trial by computer. It is this complexity, a complexity which is added to by having a specialist vocabulary and complicated procedures, which ensures that the kaffir legal expert will always be needed, and will always command a good price for his advice and services in court.

This situation is the complete antithesis of that which arises in the muslim community. The muslim community has no need of a legal system. Everything it needs is in Qur'an. Qur'an does not need to be changed because it contains guidance as to what to do in every conceivable situation in which a person may find him or her self. It already has what more enlightened legislators have been seeking to attain for the last several hundred years. Since its contents, as regards the behaviour of people within the community and the manner in which they are to conduct their affairs, are simple, it follows that there is no need whatsoever for a specialist elite to set themselves up as its interpreters or to enforce it on others. The people in a real muslim community follow what is in Qur'an because they do not wish to do otherwise. Provided they fear Allah and the Last Day, and follow the way of the prophet Muhammad and the first muslim community which gathered round him, they are not a threat to anyone else and no one is a threat to them.

One of the secrets of existence is that whatever is in your heart appears before you in existence. Since the kaffir has disorder in the heart he or she experiences disorder in existence. The kaffir then tries to put existence in order by changing it outwardly. If there is still disorder in the heart, however, the measures taken by the kaffir have no effect, and disorder merely manifests before him or her in a different form. Since the muslim, that is the one who is at peace, has peace in the heart it follows that peace manifests before the muslim in creation. The only way to change what is in your heart is to follow the way of the prophet Muhammad and the community which first gathered round him at Madina al Munawarra, that is, the illuminated place where the life transaction is. Madina was illuminated by a people whose hearts had been illuminated with knowledge and love of Allah, and who accordingly had no need of the systems which characterise the kaffir system, that is the Dajjal system, especially its kaffir legal system.

Islam is not a system. It is a way of life, and you can only be described as muslim if you follow that way. Those countries which have been colonised and subjected to the kaffir legal system and the kaffir consumer producer process cannot be described as having muslim governments, merely because a little of what is in Qur'an has been incorporated in acts of parliament. A muslim country has no need of a kaffir styled parliament. The Qur'an is its constitution. Allah says in Qur'an that there is no compulsion in the life transaction. Once you know which way to go, you simply abandon the way which was a hindrance to you. It is not enough to be called muslim. It is necessary to be muslim, that is to embody the way of Islam and to be at peace with yourself and with existence. The prophet Muhammad, may the blessings and peace of Allah be on him, said that a muslim is one from whose hand and whose tongue you are safe. He said that the muslims should be like two hands washing each other, and like the rafters of a roof which support each other. He said you are not a muslim until you want for your companion what you want for your self. He said that if you have a full stomach and someone in the house next door has an empty stomach, then you are not a muslim. He said that the best aspect of Islam is to greet those you know and those you do not know, and to welcome and feed the guest. If the people in a muslim community have this approach to life and to each other, then it follows that they are already what the kaffir describes as law abiding citizens. This is only possible in a community of people whose lives are based on worship of Allah. As has already been noted, muslim communities in the past have always disintegrated, once their members abandoned what is in Qur'an and turned away from Allah to what is other than Allah.

The offences which are formulated by the kaffir legal system are not so formulated by reference to what happens after death. This is in marked contrast to the relatively few offences against the muslim community which are indicated in Qur'an. The offences referred to in Qur'an are those anti social acts which, if freely permitted, would undermine the trust which is essential if the members of that community are to live together in harmony. The number of witnesses required before the offence may be punished means that there can be no doubt in the matter. This is in marked contrast to the kaffir legal system, where a person can be convicted and punished of any number of offences on the flimsiest of circumstancial evidence, and nearly always when a member of the police says that the person in the dock was either seen to do the act in question, or admitted to doing it at the police station. The police are highly skilled in incorporating into their written records of alleged interviews with the accused or of the alleged behaviour of the accused, admissions or acts which will guarantee a conviction once the matter comes to trial. It is an unwritten presumption of kaffir law that where there is conflict between the police version of events and the accused's version of events, then the police version is to be believed. If the presumption were the other way around then there would be too many acquittals, and as a result the kaffir legal system would not be the thriving business concern that it is today.

As far as punishment is concerned, in the kaffir legal system the motivation behind punishment is to make money, and to render ineffective those who threaten the fabric of kaffir society. In theory the punishment is regarded as the just retribution which is to be inflicted on the offender by the legal system, on behalf of the remainder of the kaffir society. The fact that a great majority of people in today's kaffir society do not agree with the law or the offender's being punished, is always conveniently overlooked by those who continue to administer the law in their name and allegedly on their behalf. The punishments inflicted in a kaffir society are also intended to deter others from following the example of the person who has been punished. Indeed by invoking that nebulous concept known as public policy, or the interests of the state, which in reality are the interests of the ruling elite who benefit most from maintaining the status quo as it is, it is possible to punish someone far more than they deserve in order that others will be sufficiently deterred from following suit. Since the punishments are in order that the status quo can be maintained, it follows that they derive from a distorted perspective.

The relatively few punishments in Qur'an are admittedly retributive and deterrent in effect, but the primary motivation behind them is that the one who submits to a Qur'anic punishment is thereby released from his or her wrong action, and accordingly may still go to the Garden. Indeed since the muslim fears Allah and longs for the Garden and dreads the Fire, it follows that he or she is far less likely to do a major wrong action in the first place. This perspective is entirely lacking in a kaffir society. The kaffir does not realise that every action is witnessed by the recording angels, and by Allah, and will have to be answered for on the Last Day. Given this ignorance, the kaffir is far more prone to do wrong action, and if he or she is then caught, will be processed by the kaffir legal system without reference to what is yet to take place on the Last Day. Allah says in Qur'an that the kaffir receives a double punishment, in this world and the next.

Since the kaffir legal system is not based on any divine revelation, other than those few laws which derive from the remnants of earlier prophetic guidances, or which tally with what is in Qur'an by sheer coincidence, but rather is formulated in defiance of such revelation, it follows that many of the offences which are defined by the kaffir legal system are offences only because they have been defined as such by ignorant men, who are not acting in accordance with what Allah has indicated should be regarded as wrong action. Many of the offences defined by the kaffir legal system are not even based on common sense, and certainly do not arise from wisdom. They have come into being because the consumer producer system needs a great many rules if it is to operate efficiently, and these rules can only be enforced by punishing the people by whom and when they are broken. They are the result of political expediency, the necessary means for effective manipulation and population control in the kaffir system, that is the Dajjal system. It will be remembered that the definition of an ignorant person is the one who thinks he or she knows, when in reality he or she does not.

Just as the kaffir medical experts have an illusory definition of what normal is, so too do the kaffir legal experts. In effect if you fulfil the functions of an obedient robot in the kaffir producer consumer system, then you fall fully within the kaffir legal definition of what is normal. Anyone who falls outside the legal norm of the kaffir system, that is the Dajjal system, soon finds him or her self in trouble with the kaffir legal system. As the kaffir police state becomes more and more of a reality, and more and more oppressive, it becomes increasingly more difficult to follow any human way of life which is a viable alternative to that norm, without experiencing greater and greater harrassment from the kaffir legal system. The kaffir legal experts, who frame the laws which make the kaffir system, that is the Dajjal system, work, are skilled in defining laws which will enable the controllers of that system to take whatever steps are necessary to protect their interests and maintain the status quo. Anyone whose action falls within the legal definition of an offence is automatically considered a criminal, and can be punished accordingly. It follows that any pattern of activity which threatens the continued existence of the kaffir system, that is the Dajjal system, can be legally destroyed or disrupted merely by passing a law which makes that pattern of activity illegal. The kaffir media system is then used to justify and promote that law by using the appropriate emotive adjectives to describe the pattern of activity which has just been outlawed, such as anarchistic, fanatical, terrorist, and by using the appropriate platitudes to make the law seem necessary, such as in the public interest, in the interests of the state, for the protection of society. The ease with which such laws can be passed is eloquent proof of the fact that the ruling elite of the kaffir system, that is the Dajjal system, are not only established at the head of all the interlinking systems which form the kaffir system, but also by virtue of that fact are able to work in close conjunction with each other.

The law making body in any kaffir state is also the body which administers those laws, is also the body which governs in purported accordance with those laws, no matter how many carefully worded theories concerning the doctine of the separation of powers there are, which seek to create the impression that the legislators, the judiciary and the executive are independent of each other, and therefore by implication incorruptible. In reality the opposite of this doctrine is true of the typical kaffir state, and that is why it is possible to legally silence anyone who is too manifestly opposed to the kaffir system, that is the Dajjal system, with ease.

As well as ensuring that the kaffir norm is upheld and maintained, the kaffir legal system, like the kaffir medical system, is big business. It is for this reason that so many prosecutions, which otherwise would be completely pointless and unnecessary, are pursued. The outcome of the prosecution is not important. Whether the person accused is convicted or acquitted is quite irrelevant. What matters, as far as the people working in the kaffir legal system are concerned, is that they are kept occupied. If they had a just society they would be out of a job, and that is why the controllers of the kaffir state ensure that they do not have a just society. As is the case with every system in the kaffir system, that is the Dajjal system, the kaffir legal system ensures its continued and profitable existence by creating work for itself. Of all the systems it is the most cannibalistic, for in effect it feeds off human beings. Even a simple motoring so called offence by one person, for example, is a potential source of income for the police who deal with him or her, the solicitor, the barrister, the judiciary, and of course all those who fill the bureaucratic positions which are necessary to enable the cumbersome machinery of the kaffir legal system to grind on its way. It is one of the surprises of creation that there are people who can view such a system with pride and love, but then every created being loves something. The fly loves shit, whilst the bee loves honey.

Given this set up it is not surprising that the police are forced by the very nature of the kaffir system, that is the Dajjal system, to hunt for and prosecute even the most trivial of so called offences and offenders. Given the presence of all the various legal entities in the kaffir legal system, it follows that they must have work to justify their existence. The vast amounts of money, which are gathered by means of fines imposed in the kaffir courts each day, are used to supplement the money gathered by means of taxes, in order to cover the running costs of the kaffir legal system. These costs are vast. The police force is continually increasing in size, and not only must its members receive their above average pay, but also they must have all the latest equipment.

Since kaffir legal procedure and kaffir laws are complex, and expressed in a specialist vocabulary, most people who find themselves accused of anything have to obtain assistance from lawyers if they are to stand any chance of acquittal in court at all. Since not all the victims of the kaffir legal system are rich, and indeed most of them come from the helpless and the poor, provision has to be made for the lawyers who represent them. The legal aid scheme ensures that the lawyers will still get paid, even when their client has no money. Naturally the handsome income of the judiciary, and the not so handsome income of the people filling the bureaucratic posts in the kaffir legal system, is safely guaranteed, but adds a great deal to the annual cost of running the kaffir legal system.

Finally there is the upkeep of the buildings in which the people who operate the kaffir legal system enact their daily drama, as well as the need to erect more buildings in what is after all a profitable and expanding business. All this expense, most of it unnecessary, has to be met by the people enslaved in the producer consumer process.

It is not only the criminal law but also the civil law which is a potential source of handsome reward for those involved in the legal system. The dependance of people on the civil law process is achieved by ensuring that even the simplest of transactions needs to be evidenced in writing if it is to be regarded as valid. When you are born, your birth must be registered, as must eventually your death. Marriage must be registered and if it does not work out, it is only by means of the civil law that it can be legally dissolved, and financial provision and division of shared assets be made. When you die your property cannot be distributed according to your wishes without going to court.

Thus all the basic features of life, that is birth, marriage and death, are in a kaffir society only regarded as real and valid and legal and right and proper, if they have been endorsed by usually quite unnecessary paper work. Further reliance on the kaffir civil legal process is also ensured by the fact that in a situation where people do not trust each other, and are suspicious of each other's motives, and this is the condition of the kaffir mind, they will place reliance on the court to obtain for them what they want. What this means is that the kaffir has to be confronted with the threat of impending punishment before he or she will keep his or her word when it does not seem expedient so to do.

By far the greatest volume of work for the kaffir civil courts derives from the consumer producer process itself. Since that process is based on competition and exploitation, it follows that there will always be people who are trying to get something for nothing, and this can usually only be achieved by clever word play which achieves the desired result without infringing the law. The guidance of a kaffir legal expert is needed in such matters. Similarly such dishonest activity can usually only be prevented by taking the matter before the courts. Allah says in Qur'an that the kaffirs appear to be one body, but they are divided against each other. It is this division, which is characterised by lack of trust and the willingness to take advantage of others, which ensures that the kaffir civil courts and lawyers are kept in business. Furthermore, because the kaffir system, that is the Dajjal system, needs so many rules and regulations in order to function, this means not only that there will always be many breaches of those rules occurring, but also that experts will be needed to interpret those rules both in their application and in dealing with breaches thereof. Further dependance on the kaffir civil judicial process is ensured by the fact that these rules are for ever changing, which means not only are the publishers of legal books given continued and lucrative work, but also that it is only the kaffir legal expert who has even the slightest idea of what the legal position is in a given situation, in any one point of time. When anything goes wrong in a kaffir transaction, the only way to ensure that things are put right is by employing the people who know how to deal with paperwork, and who have some idea of how all the laws, which govern the validity of what the paper in question records, operate. Amongst people who trust each other, neither these laws, nor the courts which administer them, nor the experts who interpret them, are necessary.

The involvement of the kaffir banking, insurance, hire purchase, building society and other finance systems in the kaffir producer consumer system that is the Dajjal system, and indeed in all aspects of people's lives lived in the context of that system, also ensure that the kaffir civil judicial process is provided with trade. All these kaffir financial institutions deal in sophisticated magic, in that they create money out of nothing by charging interest, an activity which Allah expressly prohibits in Qur'an, saying that those who indulge in it are for the Fire. They all work on the understanding that anyone, who has been adequately programmed to desire the products of the consumer producer process, will be willing to pay extra if he or she can have immediate possession of the product in question. The extra is calculated in terms of interest. Since all these finance institutions only exist to make money out of people, they are merciless in commencing legal proceedings whenever a person falls behind in payment. This situation is the complete opposite of that where one muslim lends money to another muslim, and is quite prepared to wait long beyond the agreed time of repayment, and if necessary relieve the friend of having to repay altogether, firm in the knowledge that Allah will repay the debt for him or her ten times over. Indeed there are some muslims who refuse to lend money, but will only give it away, on the principle and in the knowledge that if they lend money they only stand to regain the sum lent, whereas if they give it away they will recover ten times that amount, in accordance with the promise and by the outpouring of Allah. This knowledge is entirely lacking in the typical kaffir financial institution which, because of its size and the manner in which it is run, can be utterly ruthless with the most deserving of people, simply because the individual who is borrowing the money never meets the individual who is lending it. The representative of the kaffir financial institution is always in a position to say that if he or she could help then he or she would, but unfortunately rules are rules, and he or she is bound by the rules of the company and his or her contract of employment. Most of the transactions are conducted via computer, and, since most kaffir computers have not been programmed to be compassionate, for their programmers are not compassionate, accordingly legal proceedings can be initiated automatically and without deliberation or compassion.

Although the insurance companies are concerned primarily with safeguarding products once they have been acquired, by agreeing to pay out money to the owner if the product is lost or damaged in certain specified circumstances, and provided that the owner agrees to pay a specified premium to the insurance company throughout the period of insurance, they also play a large role in the context of personal injury and fatal accident claims. Since they are in the insurance trade solely for purposes of business, the amounts they are prepared to pay out on the various claims have already been carefully calculated, so that after they have been paid out the company will be left with an overall profit. If they can get away with paying less on a claim than they expect they will have to pay, then they will do so. This means that many claims become the subject of litigation, for it is only when experts' reports have been prepared, and lawyers employed to bargain by correspondence and advise the respective parties as to what sum the judge would be likely to award if the matter went to court, that it may become clear as to how much the claim is really worth. This pattern of activity is another clear example of how the kaffir system, that is the Dajjal system, creates activity in order that money can be made out of it.

The kaffir civil legal process is like the kaffir criminal legal process: It makes money out of other people's misfortunes. A person who breaks an arm at work because, for example, he was given a faulty ladder to use, will not receive any financial compensation for his injury until after the insurance company has been involved, solicitors and barristers have been involved, medical experts have been involved, and, if agreement cannot be reached, until the matter has been finally settled in court. In a simple case like this the costs of all these different entities being involved will be greatly in excess of the sum which is finally recovered by the victim of the accident. The truth of the matter is that this pattern of activity is not really for the benefit of the victim. It is more for the benefit of the so called experts without whose help the victim can recover nothing.

This is the key to the kaffir system, that is the Dajjal system. Once the experts who control that system have persuaded the majority of the population to rely on their services, then the position and income of the kaffir experts, and therefore the continued existence of that system, is assured.

The muslim community has no need of these so called experts. In the case of unexpected damage to property or injury to life and limb, the members of the community help each other out. Where appropriate, money can be distributed from the Bait ul Maal, that is the fund into which the members of the community pay the minimal taxes required by Qur'an. The only taxes which the muslim is liable to pay are the zakat which is a tax of two and a half per cent of any capital or income, which has been accumulated for at least a year, over and above what its owner actually needs in order to live; and a tax of two and a half per cent of merchandise; and a tax of ten per cent on naturally watered crops, or five per cent on artificially watered crops, which is to be paid in the form of one tenth or one twentieth of what has been harvested; and a tax of a small proportion of any herd of livestock over a certain size; and a tax of two and a half per cent of the value of all mineral and subterranean resources which are mined. There is also the zakat al fitr, which is four both hands cupped fulls of a local staple food, usually grain or dried fruit, payable by or on behalf of every muslim in the community at the end of Ramadan, which is the lunar month during which every adult muslim in good health fasts between dawn and sunset. Finally, if a muslim finds buried treasure, he must pay a tax on it of twenty per cent. All these taxes are paid into the Bait ul Maal.

Since the way of Islam is based on giving out, a real muslim community ensures that the contents of this central fund are distributed to those in need, as defined in Qur'an, as quickly as it fills up. Since the taxes are gathered at different times of the year, it follows that the fund is continually being filled, expended and replenished. The taxes are so simple that they can be understood by someone who is illiterate. There is thus no need for the expert to interpret and adminster them.

There are two other taxes, payable by non muslims, which are equally simple: The jizya tax, which is paid by all adult males of the ahlul dhimma, that is the non muslims living under muslim rule and protection. The amount per head, which can be reduced in cases of real poverty, is four dinars of gold or forty dirhams of silver each year. By virtue of paying the jizya tax, the ahlul dhimma do not have to fight if the muslim community is attacked, and are entitled to the protection by the muslims during such an attack. The other tax is ten per cent on imports into muslim territory from other countries, levied on traders who are not muslim.

The absolute simplicity of the muslim taxes means that they can be gathered with ease. Since they are so low everyone can afford to pay them. There is thus none of the unnecessary activity which is engendered by the kaffir tax laws, which are so complex and so oppressive that they create the demand for legal experts to interpret them and find ways of evading and avoiding them, and for a complex bureaucratic system to collect them, and of course provide the authorities with the work of catching tax offenders and the kaffir legal system with more business, in dealing with them.

It should be by now quite evident that the primary concern of the kaffir legal system is making money and creating situations from which money can be made, not justice. It follows that the outcome of a good many cases depends not on the facts or the merits of the case, but on who is going to have to pay the costs. This means that there are two laws, one for the rich and one for the poor. This means that the kaffir legal system favours those who control the kaffir system, that is the Dajjal system, at the expense of those who are enslaved by that system. The profits involved are increased by the fact that since the kaffir legal machine involves much bureaucracy there is much delay. This delay is a disadvantage to the accused or to the litigant as the case may be, since when events are no longer fresh in people's minds the outcome of the case becomes more uncertain. As far as the people who are involved with the conduct of the case are concerned however, any delay means more pay. The kaffir legal system, the heart of the kaffir system, that is the Dajjal system, creates work for itself and is given work by virtue of the way in which the kaffir producer consumer system operates, and it makes vast sums of money out of that work, whilst at the same time maintaining the status quo which ensures that that work continues to be made available.

Only those who know how the kaffir system, that is the Dajjal system, works, and who help to control it, share in the profits which arise from the way in which it operates. Everyone else loses out, in monetary terms at any rate. Of course in the final analysis success or failure can only be measured in terms of whether you end up in the Garden or in the Fire in the life after this one. If one looks at the kaffir system, that is the Dajjal system, from this Qur'anic perspective, then it is clear that the kaffir controllers, who imagine that they have got it made in this world, are in for a big shock in the next one. It follows that the following exerpt from a letter from the London banking firm of Rothschild Brothers, dated 25 June 1863 and addressed to the New York bank of Ickleheimer, Morton and Van der Gould, is only of limited accuracy when viewed from the kaffir perspective, and of no truth when viewed from the Qur'anic perspective:

> "The few who understand the system ... will either be so interested in its profits, or so dependant on its favours, that there will be no opposition from that class, while, on the other hand, the great body of people, mentally incapable of comprehending the tremendous advantages that Capital derives from the system, will bear its burden without complaint, and perhaps without even suspecting that the system is inimical to their interests ..."

It must be emphasized that the prophetic mode of existence is the complete opposite of the kaffir system that is the Dajjal system. Kufr creates complexity. Islam embodies simplicity. In the muslim community there is a complete absence of institutions and bodies of experts whose livelihood and continued existence depends on creating work for themselves, by feeding off other people's misfortunes. The prophet Muhammad, may the blessings and peace of Allah be on him, said: "We are an illiterate community. We do not write and we do not calculate." Human transactions in a muslim community are conducted on the basis of mutual trust, and not on the basis of a spurious legal validity which necessitates paper work. Qur'an contains all the guidance a human being or group of beings needs. Where disputes arise, they can be settled by reference to what is in Qur'an, and not by reference to other people's decisions in similar fact situations in the past, or to complex, arbitrary and for ever changing laws and rules. It is true that there are those who have attempted to make a legal system based on kaffir legal systems out of the teachings of Islam, but they can not be regarded as muslims and must be ignored. They are merely the fulfillment of the prophet Muhammad's observation that there would be those who, in the name of Islam, would follow the example of their predecessors, meaning the Jews and the Christians, faster than a lizard makes for its hole, that is by compromising and abandoning the guidance which their prophet had brought.

The nature of the real muslim community is such, that there can be no consumer producer process, because the muslim knows that he or she was not created for that purpose; that there can be no educational system such as is operated by the kaffir system, that is the Dajjal system, because the muslim does not need to be conditioned to be exploited, because the basis of the muslim community is worship of Allah and not the exploitation of others, and also the knowledge which the muslim has is certain knowledge derived from Qur'an, and directly from Allah, and not the useless and speculative information in which the kaffir educational system largely traffics; that there can be no medical system, because the muslim by virtue of his or her way of life is healthy and when sick, uses a different form of healing to that employed by the kaffir medical system; that there can be no legal system, because the guidance in Qur'an is complete and does not need to be changed, and because anyone can follow it without the necessity of experts to interpret it, and because it can only be followed if it is accepted voluntarily and not if it is inflicted on others; that there can be no financial systems which operate on the basis of charging interest, because not only are these forbidden by Allah, but also because muslim economics is based on generosity and giving out, and not on being mean and retention.

In a real muslim society there are no faceless institutions, there are no banks as we know banks today, there are no prisons and no law courts, there is no police force, or standing army for that matter. The ruler is the person whom everyone has accepted as their ruler, and who follows what is in Qur'an. Since there is no ruling elite, for the way of Muhammad expressly forbids dynastic rule and whoever adopts dynastic rule does so in defiance of the guidance sent by Allah, it follows that there is no body of people who, because they wish to exploit the rest of the population, need to have the means of oppression and the means which are used to disguise the nature of that oppression.

Whenever anyone in a muslim community goes beyond the bounds of Allah, as indicated in Qur'an, in a manner which harms someone else or the community as a whole, then that person is dealt with, in accordance with what is in Qur'an by the community through its leader and on the spot without delay. No one in a muslim community can be deprived of their liberty for more than three days, no matter what they may have done. Everyone inclines to wrong action at some time or other. The compassionate way in which the prophet Muhammad dealt with those who had gone beyond the bounds set by Allah provides a clear example of how to rule, for all those who have been chosen to rule. He directed rulers not to reach a conclusion until they had heard both sides of the story, and not to sit in judgement if they were angry or constipated. The fact that anything which occurs is dealt with on the spot means that there is no room for bureaucracy or bureaucrats or paper work. In a muslim community justice is not a matter of who pays the costs, because there are no costs of the kind which the operation of the kaffir systems engenders to pay.

Everyone in a muslim community who has taken upon him or her self the obligations of the sharia, that is the road to Allah, which are simply stated in Qur'an, and who fears Allah and the Last Day, is solely by virtue of the way in which he or she has chosen to live neither a threat to others nor to his or her own self. To follow the prophetic life style is to live in harmony with one's self and with others, and in order to achieve this balance there is no need whatsoever for a body of people who have appointed themselves as the judges of others' actions and as the enforcers of this way of life. Indeed whenever this group appears, and there is always a time when it does, it is a sign of disintegration, a sign of the first inclination away from Islam towards Kufr. The whole point of the way of Islam is that it cannot be successfully imposed on anyone who does not wish to follow it. It can only be voluntarily adopted by the one who wishes to live in that way. Allah says in Qur'an that there is no compulsion in the life transaction. Only a fool tries to force people to live in a certain manner, for the reality of existence is that every atom is in its place, and everything that takes place is intended by Allah. If you look at creation you can find no crack in it. It is perfect. If you are a muslim it is no good trying to be a kaffir. If you are a kaffir it is no good trying to be a muslim. You can only be who you are and allow others to be who they are. There is no power and no strength except from Allah.

Continual reference has been made to the ruling elite of the kaffir system that is the Dajjal system, and to the fact that they now control all the sub-systems which together make up that system. Up to now this group of kaffir controllers has not been positively identified. It is now necessary to take a closer look at who they are.

Co-ordinated control of the apparently separate albeit interlinking sub systems which together form the kaffir system, that is the Dajjal system, is made possible by the existence of the ruling elite's secret organizations, the various lodges of the free masons. The ruling elite of the kaffir system, that is the Dajjal system, are the free masons. Their activities are masked by the popular misconception that the free masons are no more than a fraternity who help each other in the business world. That is true, but the extent of that mutual assistance, and the high degree of influence and control which they exercise, is hidden from public knowledge.

The hierarchy within these lodges, as is typical of all kaffir systems, is pyrammidical in form. One of their symbols is the pyramid with the seeing eye, the eye of Dajjal. The free masons are the magicians of the twentieth century. All magic is concerned with a formal manipulation of existence which is conducted in such a way that the method used to achieve the desired result is not apparent to the onlooker. This accurately describes the nature of free masonic activity in the sphere of the kaffir producer consumer system, that is the Dajjal system, even to the point where governments are subverted and wars engineered in order that debts may be created, by supplying so called advisers and arms at a cost, which is further inflated by the fact that interest is charged on the debts thereby incurred.

The free masons are today's equivalent of Pharaoh's magicians, many of whom, as we know from Qur'an, supported the kaffir manipulation control system of Pharaoh, which opposed Moses and his teaching, and which eventually brought about its own downfall by so doing. The story of the transaction between Moses and Pharaoh is related in great detail and more than once in Qur'an. It demonstrates with great clarity that when a man of Allah, who knows that he is completely helpless in the hands of Allah, meets a man of Kufr, who relies on the magic which Allah has given him without his knowing it, then it is the man of Allah to whom victory is given by Allah. There is no strength and no power except from Allah. The transaction between Moses and Pharaoh is the same transaction as that between Noah and the kaffir ruler of his time, is the same transaction as that between Abraham and Nimrod, is the same transaction as that between Jesus and the Roman Emperor, is the same transaction as that between Muhammad and Abu Jahl, is the same transaction as that which today occurs between Iman and Kufr, and which will find its final expression in the confrontation between the Mahdi and Dajjal.

Looking at history from the Qur'anic perspective, we see that there has only ever been one major transaction between people on the face of this earth, that is the transaction between those who accept Allah and His prophets and those who reject Allah and His prophets.

Allah is as He was before the creation of the Universe and continues to be. Allah is as He will be. Allah can not be conceived of, and everything other than Allah which appears to be is the conception of Allah. Vision cannot contain Him, but He contains vision, and he is the All Pervading, the Knower of every separate thing that befalls us. Allah is One. Allah is independant of what appears to be other than Allah. He was not born from anything and nothing is born from Him and there is nothing like Him. There is no god only Allah. There is only Allah. All the prophets and messengers of Allah were sent by Allah to teach people the meaning of these words, and to show them how to live in accordance with that meaning. They were sent in order that people might know the nature of reality that is the Real that is Allah, and in order that people might know how to live with that knowledge. They were sent with a way of life which would lead those who followed it to self knowledge and to knowledge of Allah, the same knowledge, for who ever knows their self truly knows their Lord. It follows that all the prophets' teachings were essentially the same, although differing in accordance with the needs of the time for which each was meant, since they came from and affirmed the same and only One Reality, Allah. It follows that the people who have lived or live or are to live on this earth have only ever had or will have one choice, that is whether to be Mumin or Kaffir. In Reality there is not even that choice, since you can only be what Allah has decreed you to be. Allah is the doer of you and your actions. You are answerable for your actions. On the Last Day you will not question Allah, but Allah will question you. Right now the choice is yours.

Dajjal is not something separate from Kufr. Dajjal is the final and most extreme expression of Kufr before the end of the world, just as the Mahdi will be the final and most eloquent embodiment of Islam before the end of the world. It will be remembered that the Mahdi will be a drop compared to the ocean of the prophet Muhammad, may the peace and blessings of Allah be on him. It is the final confrontation between the Mahdi and the Dajjal and their respective followers which, according to the Hadith, heralds the end of the world. During that final confrontation the prophet Jesus will reappear on earth and kill Dajjal. There will then follow the peaceful rule of the Mahdi as leader of all the Muslims, who will be spread all round the world. After this period there will come a time when Allah will take the arwah, that is the spirit forms, of all those who trust in Allah from their bodies and this earth, so that there is only one Muslim left on the face of the earth, in China. When he dies, there will be a period when those who are left on the earth will live like animals. At the end of this period, Israfil the angel will blow the first blast of his trumpet, at which every living thing will die. The earth will remain lifeless for a period. At the end of this period Israfil will give a second blast on his trumpet at which the world will disintegrate, as is described in Qur'an, until it has become one vast flat plain of silver sand. All those who have ever lived will be brought to life again, and this is easy for the One who gave you life in the first place. Then, depending on their actions and the intentions behind those actions whilst they were in this world, it will be decided who is for the Fire, and who is for the Garden. The Fire is for the Kaffirs. The Garden is for the Muslims. Dajjal and his followers are for the Fire. The Mahdi and his followers are for the Garden. You are either for the Fire or for the Garden. Right now the choice is yours.

The free masons are the leaders of the take over by Dajjal as an unseen force. Their activities are evidenced by Dajjal as a world wide social and cultural phenomenon. They will be the ones who acclaim and support Dajjal the individual when he appears. Without the free masons the take over would not have progressed as far as it has today. Since, at the moment of writing this, they control all the kaffir institutions and systems in the world today, it would seem that they have never been in an apparently stronger position than now to orchestrate their plans for world domination through the producer consumer process and backed by their banking system, by means of dividing and ruling. The point has even been reached where they are planning mass sterilization of women in the third world countries so that they can manipulate and balance the forces of supply and demand in the world market. The high degree of control exercised by them today is witnessed by the fact that they are able to instigate a war, provide the arms for the two sides to be able to fight it, at a price of course, and then take over control, or strengthen control if they already have it, once the fighting is over, any opposition to them having been considerably weakened by the inevitable consequences of war.

This technique of manipulation control by divide and rule is effected by operating on two fronts at the same time. There is what goes on behind the scenes as it were, and there is the official stage production which is put on for the benefit of the general public. The manner in which the hidden activities are conducted is highly ruthless, and the efficiency with which they are carried out is matched only by the lengths to which the free masons are prepared to go to put on a convincing constitutional, legal and just stage production for the benefit and continued misguidance of the unsuspecting public. The success of the show, that is of the official version of events, is only made possible by the fact that the different kaffir sub systems are able to interlink and co-operate, by virtue of the fact that they are controlled by one and the same ruling elite, the free masons, who staged the french revolution to begin with, and who have never ceased to increase the magnitude of their stage productions and the control underlying them since that time.

The interaction of the medical and legal kaffir systems provides perhaps the most eloquent example of the free masonic co-operation which is necessary to ensure a good stage production fronting the acquisition of ultimate control. It is not a coincidence that, taking London as an example, the High Court of Justice and the Royal College of Surgeons have their backs facing each other, but are separated only by a stone's throw. Although they apparently face in different directions, they work in close conjunction with each other when necessary. To give but two examples of how the legal and

49

medical kaffir systems, aided of course by the kaffir media system, work together, we may examine the trial of Ezra Pound, the famous poet, and the Nuremberg trials, both of which took place immediately after the second kaffir world war.

Ezra Pound was only too well aware that what passed itself off as education in the western world was nothing less than a conditioning process which guaranteed ignorance of the overall nature and unity of existence, at the expense of being highly informed about specific and isolated pockets of life, the height of that ignorance being the person who thinks he or she knows all there is to know, when in fact the opposite is the case. He was also only too well aware that both the first and second kaffir world wars had been engineered, precipitated and orchestrated by the free masons, who as a result had made much money out of them, as well as increasing their control over and in not only the governments of all the countries involved, but also their educational, business, medical, legal and media systems, thereby ensuring and insuring, via their banking, insurance and other finance systems, virtually complete control over much of the kaffir producer consumer process which was being established in those countries.

Ezra Pound was brave enough to broadcast what he saw was going on over the radio from Italy midway during the second kaffir world war. He was foolish or foolhardy enough not to realise the degree of control which the free masons already exercised over the systems which he hoped to liberate by warning the people of the danger which threatened to engulf them, and by suggesting an alternative way of life and of government and commerce, based on the teachings of Confucius, which at the time he was in the process of translating. It would appear that he was unaware of the only viable alternative way of life to the kaffir system that is the Dajjal system, that is the way of Muhammad.

When the American forces reached the part of Italy where Pound was, he was immediately arrested. At that point he imagined that he was going to be taken to America to advise the government as to how to best adopt and implement the Confucian mode into the American way of life. The basis of this mode echoed the resolve of the original founding fathers of America, in that interest in any form or guise should not be charged on any kind of debt or loan. Pound's subsequent treatment soon demonstrated that he was sadly mistaken in his belief, and showed how inimicable the controlling free masonic elite of

America were to any suggestions which threatened their chief source of revenue and control, that is the creation of debts and the charging of interest thereon, so that the debtors had no choice but to work continuously in their producer consumer process, in order to raise the money to pay off the old debts, whilst at the same time incurring fresh ones. The take over had already been virtually completed in America, and accordingly as far as the ruling elite of America was concerned, Ezra Pound was public enemy number one.

Soon after his arrest, Pound was taken to Pisa, where he was put in solitary confinement in an iron cage which stood out in the middle of a military compound, and which provided no shelter from the sun by day, or from the cold of night, or from the wind and the rain. No one was allowed to hold a conversation with him. Eventually he became so ill that he had to be put inside a tent in order that he be kept alive. After several weeks he was transported to America, still suffering from exposure and ill health. On arrival in America he was given no time to recover, but was immediately brought before a judge and charged with treason, the very charge which Pound had been levelling at the free masons, since in his opinion they were destroying and corrupting the America which the original founding fathers had envisaged, and were, through their manipulation control techniques, establishing the America which in fact exists today.

Ezra Pound was not permitted to have the defence lawyer of his own choosing. Instead he was allocated a lawyer who was himself a free mason, as was the judge who presided over the judicial proceedings, and as were the medical experts who were appointed both by the prosecution and the defence lawyers.

As far as the free masons were concerned, it was important that Pound should not give evidence, nor indeed come to trial, since this would mean that his knowledge of the take over would become known to all those who followed the trial, and might become too well publicized, even though the main kaffir media systems were, and still are, controlled by the free masons. Anyone who has attempted to set up their own broadcasting station in a kaffir country will know just how tight this control exercised by the free masons is. Accordingly Pound's lawyer advised him that the best tactic was to avoid the danger of his being convicted for treason, which is an offence carrying the death penalty, by maintaining that he was unfit to stand trial by reason of insanity. In order for this stratagem to succeed, it was necessary that Pound did not speak a word in court. Pound, who was already an ageing and, because of the treatment which he had just received, a sick man, submitted to the pressure exerted by his lawyer and his wife, and agreed to adopt this approach.

Pound appeared before the judge and a grand jury on his arraignment, his lawyer made the submission that Pound was unfit to stand trial, and the judge ordered a medical enquiry to be undertaken by medical experts who were to be selected by both the prosecution and the defence lawyers. It is usual in such cases for the medical experts to disagree violently, since they are only usually selected by the respective sides in the case because their opinion is going to support and strengthen the arguments put forward by the lawyer who chose them. It would have been expected in this case therefore, that the medical experts chosen by the prosecution would have come to the conclusion that Pound was perfectly sane and fit to stand trial. However, because it had already been agreed behind the scenes what was to happen to Pound, it came as no surprise that the prosecution medical experts, who like the defence medical expert, all the lawyers concerned and the judge, were free masons, instead of supporting the contention that Pound was fit to plead and should not be allowed to escape the so called demands of justice, in fact agreed completely with the defence medical expert in stating, once the necessary but unnecessary rigmarole of due observation, examination and psychiatric tests had been performed, that Pound was indeed insane and therefore unable to stand trial. This decision was of course portrayed by the free masonic controlled media as an example of the humane treatment which a person, who could not really be held to be responsible for what he said or did, could expect to receive from a just and understanding legal system. In reality the free masons were making very sure that what Pound had said or done to expose them did not become common knowledge.

Once the medical experts had come to their inevitable conclusion, and once that conclusion had been given weight by voicing it in the correct judicial setting, Pound's committal to an insane asylum for an indefinite period was a mere formality. The free masons, as a result of the skilful and polished use and combination of their medical and legal systems, had succeeded in silencing one of their most eloquent and knowledgeable opponents with utmost ease, and all with the appearance of complete what is called legality and due judicial process. The Pound pantomime had been a resounding success: The audience were satisfied and unaware of what had really been going on.

Ezra Pound spent the next fifteen years in an insane asylum. He was allowed visitors, and indeed attracted quite a cult following, but his views were still effectively curtailed. He knew that if spoke out again, and attempted to organise a more widespread dissemination of his political views by means of his visitors, then he would either be no longer allowed to have visitors, or else he would be brought back to court, adjudged sane, and immediately put on trial for treason. He by now must have realised that he could be found guilty of treason and sentenced to death as easily as he had already been found insane and unfit to stand trial. Perhaps he saw that there was very little he could do at his advanced age, and acting virtually alone, to change the system. He had tried to kill the many headed monster by cutting off one or two of its heads, and failed. He was probably unaware of the way to its heart. He chose to remain alive and be a celebrated poet.

Throughout all these goings on, the free masonic controlled media discredited Pound by all possible means, fully endorsing his so called insanity, and subtly casting doubt on any of his views concerning politics and the way in which the kaffir system, that is the Dajjal system, was, and still is, being controlled. The media presented the public with the picture of a man who was a mad but gifted poet, who in his own funny way was competent in this sphere of literary activity, but who was otherwise totally inadequate and unqualified to make any relevant observation whatsoever on the way in which America was being governed and controlled by the free masons, not only by means of their banking, insurance and other finance systems, but also through all the large kaffir institutions and systems, whether business, educational, media, medical, legal, or governmental.

All efforts were made to ensure that Pound's views were given as restricted a circulation as possible. Since the free masons controlled the publishing world, which not only provides the kaffir educational system with all its ammunition, but also makes sure that the bookshops are filled with suitably opiate material for public consumption, nearly all of Pound's writings which attacked the kaffir system, that is the Dajjal system, with an accuracy which was a little too uncomfortable to be tolerated, were successfully withdrawn from the market. Only his pretty poems were allowed to have continued general circulation. Even today many of the editions of Pound's Cantos have certain passages blacked out, whenever sensitive areas are, or rather were, mentioned.

Finally, after fifteen years, when Pound was no longer capable of being a threat to the kaffir system, that is the Dajjal system, simply because he was old and worn out and preparing for death, he was released from the insane asylum. He returned to Italy where he subsequently died. If you ask anyone today who Ezra Pound was, they will probably tell you, a famous poet. Hardly anyone knows his real story, simply because it is very well hidden in the kaffir information retrieval systems, and not available for all and sundry. The way in which Pound was effectively silenced was only possible because of the efficient interlink which existed, and continues to exist, between the American governmental, legal, medical and media kaffir systems, an interlink which is made a reality by virtue of the control exercised by the free masons.

It is clear that the success of the performance of the kaffir stage production, which is used to disguise the true nature of the free masonic ruling elite's ruthless manipulation control techniques, depends on the acceptance by the general population of the kaffir definitions of what is normal and what is legal.

The kaffir medical experts define what is normal and what is abnormal, that is what is to be considered sane or insane. The kaffir legal experts define what is legal and what is illegal, that is what action is to be considered permissible or not permissible. Since the kaffir expert is concerned with reputation and the opinion of others, it follows that there is always more than one current definition of what is normal and what is legal, because the person who can come up with what the kaffir calls an original idea or two thereby ensures a good position in the kaffir experts' hierarchy, provided he or she is given suitable publicity and enough of it. However, although the kaffir definitions of what is normal and what is legal differ widely, they all have one basic characteristic in common, that is that they all uphold the kaffir view of existence. This means in effect that the apparent differences in opinion amongst the kaffir experts are only surface conflicts. In fact they are all agreed when it comes to rejecting the way of the prophets and affirming the way of the kaffir system, that is the Dajjal system. Kufr is one system. The kaffirs appear to be one body, but they are divided against each other.

The kaffir educational system is used to inculcate and condition the general population with the definitions which have been framed by the kaffir experts. The media is used to support and sustain this conditioning. It is for this reason that alternative ways of education which do not support the kaffir view of existence are illegal. It is a criminal offence in most kaffir states not to send your child through the kaffir educational conditioning process. If the kaffir authorities discover families who have slipped through the net, they have wide powers to take the children into what they call care, so that the children can no longer be deprived of their conditioning. Since it often happens that the parents who try to save their children from the kaffir educational system do not themselves know what its alternative is, the task of the kaffir care authorities is made easier, in satisfying the kaffir court that the children should be taken into care because the parents cannot cope. Similarly, the most influential media systems, that is radio and television, are monopolised by the kaffir system that is the Dajjal system. It is a criminal offence in most kaffir states to make an independant radio or television broadcast without a licence. Only those organisations which support the kaffir system are likely to be granted such a licence. In this way penetrating cricitism of the kaffir system that is the Dajjal system on a mass basis is effectively prevented. Instead limited coverage is given to the extremists, since its effect is to persuade the average viewer or listener that the apparent relative stability of the kaffir system, that is the Dajjal system, is preferable to the world envisaged by the angry man, whose views are presented in the worst possible light on the kaffir media system.

Naturally all the imperfections of the kaffir system cannot be hidden from every one, and accordingly the kaffir media system presents programs in which it appears not only that these failings have been noticed and are being criticised, but also that something is being done about remedying them. These programs alternate with dream and fantasy programs. Having been shocked by the news you are then consoled by music and drama, and titillated by competition time.

The effect of the kaffir media system is to make life a cerebral affair. All the action goes on in your head via the radio or the television. It is a form of hypnosis. The result of being plugged into the kaffir media system for too long is that in the end you will accept almost anything, without actually doing anything about it, provided that your stomach is full and your bed warm. The individual in the kaffir society is bombarded with so much information by the kaffir media system, that in the end he or she is usually left feeling completely helpless when confronted with the idea of changing the system, even when he or she has a pretty good idea of how it works. There are many people in today's kaffir societies who are not at all happy with the way their lives are being organised, but who feel powerless to change either themselves or their environment. There are also those who, as a result of their kaffir educational and media conditioning, accept the world which they are presented with by that conditioning without question.

By controlling the educational and media systems, the kaffir ruling elite ensure that their definitions of what is normal and what is legal prevail. The people in a kaffir state are presented with these definitions from birth to death. Many of them only see what they are told to see. Very few realise how deeply implanted these definitions are in their consciousness, or seek to find the real meaning of existence, which is covered over by these definitions. The result of a kaffir education, that is the view of existence which comes with and as a result of it, is kufr, is what might be called the Dajjal mentality.

All these kaffir definitions are not based on an understanding of the true nature of existence. Indeed they are used to cover up the truth of things. They do not originate from prophetic revelation, which derives from the source of existence and the destination to which all existence returns, Allah. Indeed it is only by basing one's life on prophetic revelation, that is both one's existential life pattern as well as one's understanding of the nature of life itself, and today the only prophetic revelation which is still intact and available to the seeker of knowledge is Qur'an, that it is possible to cut through the web of kaffir conditioning which covers over real knowledge, that is knowledge of the Real, Allah.

The only way to base one's life on what is in Qur'an is by finding a community of muslims who most nearly follow the example and life style of the people who were the first to base their lives on what is in Qur'an, that is the first muslim community of Madina al Munawarra, which means the illuminated place where the life transaction is, who formed round the prophet Muhammad fourteen hundred years ago. Allah says in Qur'an that this was the best community which has ever been on the face of the earth, and since all creation is from Allah, He knows what He is talking about. The companions of the prophet Muhammad received their knowledge of Allah, and of how to live, by keeping company with the prophet Muhammad, whose every action embodied what is in Qur'an, whose every word contained wisdom, and whose very presence transformed and illuminated those who were near him.

The transaction of the real muslim community is the same today. The people in their community receive their learning and knowledge by the baraka, that is the blessing of their leader, who is a man of Allah and who is guided by Allah. Such a man is called a wali Allah, that is a friend of Allah. He loves Allah and Allah loves him, and the people who also love Allah and whom Allah loves gather round him. There is no competition between the awliya of Allah. Each has his or her own station with Allah. The greater the wali's fear of Allah, the higher his or her station is with Allah. The greatest of the awliya meet and talk with the prophet Muhammad in the Unseen, either in dreams or in vision. They accordingly have an access to the living life transaction of Islam which those who lay claim to leadership, merely by virtue of the fact that they have read more books than anyone else, do not have. Living Islam is not to be found in books. It is transmitted from person to person. However this transmission is only possible because the muslims have Qur'an, which means a recitation. The key to understanding what is in Qur'an is to recite it out loud, neither too soft nor too strong, either in a gathering or alone, with your attention on your heart.

The Qur'an is the uncreated word of Allah. It is the only book on the face of the earth today which has not been written by man, but which was revealed by Allah via the angel Gabriel to the prophet Muhammad, who himself could neither read nor write, and which has not been changed by one letter since it was revealed. Allah has promised that the Qur'an will be preserved intact until the end of the world.

In the light of Qur'an the kaffir definitions of the kaffir experts are seen to be what they are: ignorant and inaccurate ideas based on speculation and without certainty. The contents of the Qur'an can be used to ascertain the accuracy of any statement, since Qur'an is the definitive collection of statements on the true nature of existence, coming as it does from the Source of all existence. The more enlightened and sincere scientists from the west are discovering that all that they have purported to discover is corroborated by what is in Qur'an, and further that there is much in Qur'an which they have not yet discovered, and which they can never hope to discover, since their methods are too gross and clumsy and misconceived, to make such discoveries.

Everything in creation has meaning, but the kaffir definitions obscure and cover over what this meaning is. Since the kaffir has no certainty but only speculation, the kaffir definitions are for ever being re-defined. The kaffir experts cover up the inadequacy of their definitions by grandly stating that these definitions are changing because they are continually evolving and progressing, not because they are inadequate and misinformed. A leading kaffir proponent of the big bang theory was once asked what there was before the big bang took place. He replied that there was an unwritten agreement amongst all kaffir scientists not to ask that question, let alone to attempt to answer it. The truth is, behind this unwritten agreement, that they all know that if they admitted their ignorance, they would lose their professional titles and their salary and their reputation. The best of them know that if they really wanted to discover the true nature of existence then they would have to leave their laboratories, and seek out a man or woman of Allah, that is a person with real knowledge.

One of the key speculative theories of the present kaffir so called civilisation is the Darwinian theory of evolution. The verbal progressions of this theory have been borrowed by most kaffir theorists at some time or other to support their ideas. Basically the theory is used to further the kaffir doctrine of progress and development in all spheres of kaffir activity. Any course of action or development in technology, for example, which on the face of it is clearly suicidal, is validated by saying that it is what has evolved from what came before it, and therefore it must be better.

The part of Darwin's theory which has received most publicity is the proposition that man is not descended from Adam, but from the apes. We learn from Qur'an that the opposite is the truth. All mankind comes from Adam and Eve, despite what the kaffir geneticists may say. There was a people in the past, who rejected the messenger whom Allah had sent to them, and who, instead of following the life pattern which he had brought, lived like animals. As a result Allah turned them into apes. When Allah wishes something to happen, He says Be-It Is. Allah says in Qur'an that a people who do not follow the prophetic life pattern destroy themselves. Even a cursory examination of today's present kaffir societies plainly proves this to be the case. These kaffir societies are not evolving and getting better. They are getting worse as they disintegrate. Everything in existence is subject to birth and death, and to growth and decay. When the present kaffir system, that is the Dajjal system, disintegrates and finally collapses, the survivors will have no option but to embrace Islam, if they have not already done so.

The prophet Muhammad, may the blessings and peace of Allah be on him, said that there would not be an age which was not worse than the one before it, until the end of the world. If anything, therefore, the world and what is in it is not evolving but rather devolving. It is approaching its end. The prophet Muhammad said that you should not be children of this world, but rather children of the next world, because this world is leaving you and the next world is approaching you. The kaffir experts, who supply the kaffir definitions of what is normal and what is legal, are incapable of giving this kind of advice, simply because they are totally unaware of the true nature of the journey which we all have to make, willingly or unwillingly. They do not know from where they come, and they do not know to where they are going, and their paltry definitions amply reflect their ignorance. Surely we come from Allah, and to Allah we surely return.

The end to which these kaffir definitions are used is not to further man's understanding of the nature of existence, but is rather population manipulation and control in the kaffir producer consumer process. These definitions are used in effect to programme and condition people into accepting this kaffir process as being the meaning of their lives, and the reason for their existence. Allah says in Qur'an that He did not create man and jinn except to worship Him. As has been seen from the example of Ezra Pound, these kaffir definitions also provide the means by which the free masonic kaffir ruling elite can eliminate or at least control those human beings who recognise the kaffir system that is the Dajjal system for what it is, by subjecting them to judicial and medical processes which the majority of the population have been conditioned to accept as legal and normal.

The kaffir experts who frame and sustain these kaffir definitions are clearly identified by the descriptions contained in Qur'an as being the mufsidoon, that is the people who say they are putting everything right, when in fact they are only creating disruption, division and dissension. Thus although the actual word Dajjal does not appear in Qur'an, the activities of Dajjal, the last and ultimate expression of kufr in the creational process before the end of the world, are clearly indicated and identified. The kaffir system as a whole, with all its interlinking sub systems, all controlled by their free masonic kaffir so called experts, and the prophet Muhammad said that kufr is one system, is Dajjal as a world wide social and cultural phenomenon. The way in which the kaffir producer consumer process is operated, the way in which its supporting kaffir systems are used to control and manipulate the people enslaved by the producer consumer system, is clear evidence of the takeover which has been and is taking place by Dajjal as an unseen force. The kaffir system that is the Dajjal system dominates nearly all of the countries of the world today, and it can only be a matter of time before Dajjal the individual appears.

Another example of the manner in which the Dajjal system operates as regards the elimination of opposition by so called constitutional means is to be found in the manner in which the famous Nuremberg trials were conducted. This particular stage production was perhaps one of the most thoroughly and carefully orchestrated cover ups in the history of the Dajjal take over, and cost millions of pounds.

Hitler, like Pound, was well aware of the free masons' activities, as were his immediate followers. He instigated a widespread propaganda campaign designed to reveal these activities. He even embarked on the second world war. Like Pound he under estimated the degree of control already exercised by the free masons. There was even a stage when he believed that the American government would support him, so little did he know of the take over which had been going on in earnest in that country for at least the fifty years prior to the commencement of the second kaffir world war. What Hitler did not realise was that he was just the man that the free masons were looking for. He had sufficient charisma to attract a large enough following who would be prepared to fight for him, and he was sufficiently greedy for power and sufficiently ruthless in the methods which he was prepared to use to try and attain the power which he desired, for the free masons to be able to discredit him entirely once the war was over. In effect Hitler was used by the free masons to bring about his own destruction, whilst at the same time providing them with the situation from which they could make handsome profits out of the war, and from which they could eventually increase their control on a world wide basis.

The second kaffir world war provided nearly every country after the war with sufficient reason to amass vast quantities of armaments, thereby providing the free masons with countless potential conflict situations to exploit, for it is inevitable that once a country has arms there is going to emerge someone who wants to use them. That someone is given backing by the free masons, who also help the people opposed to that someone, on the understanding that the winner of the conflict will then return past favours, usually by purchasing more arms, borrowing money on interest, and giving free masonic backed corporations favourable contracts, to establish the kaffir producer consumer process in the country in question, and to exploit its natural resources. Since the free masons back both sides in the conflict, without either of the two sides realising it, the outcome of the conflict is immaterial, since the free masons cannot lose, whichever side wins.

As with Pound, the free masons had to come up with an effective counter move at the end of the second kaffir world war in order to effectively discredit Hitler's ideas, by portraying him as a man who was so insane that nothing which he had said could possibly be believed to have contained any truth. Having used Hitler to create a profitable conflict situation, the free masons had to then disassociate themselves not only from any involvement in his rise and downfall and the overall orchestration of the war, but also from the many truths which were undoubtedly voiced by Hitler concerning their activities. Since Hitler was himself a kaffir, this task was relatively simple. Although Hitler was aware of the free masons' bid for world control, he did not have access to the only viable alternative to the kaffir system, that is the Dajjal system, that is trust in Allah, and a way of life based on the way of life embodied by the prophet Muhammad, and followed by the community which formed around him at Madina al Munawarra, that is the illuminated place where the life transaction is. Indeed Hitler did not even have any of the ideals which Ezra Pound had possessed. Like the free masons, all that he wanted was power. In effect Hitler wished to beat the free masons at their own game, by replacing their pyrammidical power structure with his own pyrammidical power structure.

In the final analysis the second kaffir world war was merely a power struggle between kaffir powers, and not a confrontation between iman and kufr, that is a struggle between those who accept the wisdom of the prophetic lifestyle and those who reject it, although of course there were individuals on both sides, who found themselves unwillingly swept up in the conflict, and whose only way of keeping sane was by trusting in Allah. There was even one muslim colonel from Hyderabad who decided to fight for the English on the basis that if the Germans won the war, they would be so efficient in running the kaffir system, that is the Dajjal system, that it would take twice as long for it to reach the state of collapse which it has now reached today. Allah says in Qur'an that although the kaffirs appear to be one body, they are divided against each other.

Since Hitler was unaware of the degree of control which the free masons already exercised over the western world, he was foolish enough to imagine that he could succeed in his power bid for world domination. The free masons on the other hand, knew that they would win the war even before they pushed Hitler into starting it. The only losers were the people foolish enough to fight in it. The free masons' main concern was the cover up job which it was essential should be performed once the war was over. Their task was twofold. Firstly it was necessary to discredit Hitler's views on free masonic meddling and manipulation in world affirs, by bringing them into utter disrepute. Secondly it was necessary to create the impression that the actions which arose as a result of those views were other than what they really were. His views had to be reduced to the imaginings of a mad man, and accordingly without any basis of truth or accuracy. His actions, and the actions of those who followed him, had to be portrayed as the horrifying manifestation of the insane prejudices of a racially prejudiced tyrant, rather than the misguided attempts of a man who was trying to free Europe from the stranglehold control of the free masons, but unfortunately using the wrong methods.

Many of Hitler's views were either derived from, or reinforced by, the discovery and publication of the Protocols of the Elders of Zion, a small book which gives a partial yet highly informative picture of the free masonic plan for world control. The contents of the book merely reinforced what Hitler had already observed in the way of free masonic control by what he called the dictatorship of the World Stock Exchange, the monopoly of raw materials, the control of land if not its ownership and, above all, usury in all its forms.

The free masons, who at that stage of the take over had already gained almost complete control of the media in the western world, entered a highly energetic cover up campaign designed not only to establish the idea that the Protocols were a forgery, but also, and more important, to affirm that there was no truth in the contents of the Protocols whatsoever. Newspaper articles to this effect appeared in all the leading publications of the western world, and indeed still continue to appear occasionally today. The two most popular stories as to the origins of the Protocols were, firstly, that they could be traced back to a satirical dialogue between Machiavelli and Montesquieu in hell, aimed at Napoleon III, and published as part of the German novel Biarritz; and, secondly, that they were alleged to have been composed by members of the Russian secret police in Paris during the last few years of the nineteenth century, and who had drawn their ideas from a French pamphlet by a French lawyer called Maurice Joly. This cover up campaign culminated in the matter being taken before a Swiss free masonic controlled court, which duly gave the desired declaration, for the benefit of the Swiss Israelitic Alliance and the Israelitic Congregation in Berne, and indeed for the benefit of free masons in general, that the Protocols were a deliberate forgery, probably originating in the Paris Offices of the Russian Political Police, and meant for use by the Tsarist government against Russian liberals. The reader will have to satisfy him or her self as to where the truth lies, by reading the Protocols, if that is possible. As in the case of Pound's writings, the free masons who control the publishing business and its distribution outlets have ensured that virtually all copies of the Protocols and any translations thereof have long been withdrawn from the market for public consumption.

Similarly the writings of Alfred Rosenberg, who was one of Hitler's men and who wrote extensively on the Protocols, and who amongst other things traced the sources of the Russian Revolution back to free masonic activity, were withdrawn from the general public's gaze. As well as withdrawing all written records of Hitler's views which were damaging to the image of the free masons, literally hundreds of books, backed by other media presentations on radio and on the screen, were written and broadcasted in order to distort what Hitler had actually been saying. Very few people today know what Hitler actually said or believed. His views have been covered up by a barrage of emotional invective, which has prevented the vast majority of people today from actually cooly and critically examining what he had to say, and seeing what truth there was in his words. If you ask people today what motivated Hitler in his actions, most of them will give a predictable involuntary shiver, and dutifully come out with the free masonic media manufactured picture of a tyrant who was irrationally prejudiced against the Jews, for no reason other than that they were Jews. There is no doubt that Hitler did hate the Jews, but he did have his reasons, and some of them were good ones.

As far as Hitler's actions and the actions of those who followed him were concerned, they were clearly excessive, and this made it all the easier for the free masons to portray them as being far more excessive than they really were. It is always easier to exaggerate something that has happened, than to manufacture something which never even happened at all. The free masons took full advantage of this fact in their attempts to depict Hitler and his followers as racialist madmen, who wished to destroy the Jews and establish the Aryan master race. Using highly emotive techniques of media manipulation, which include the display of the incriminating close up, but not the overall picture, backed up by highly loaded vocabulary, the free masons were highly successful in portraying Hitler as a disordered psychopath, who was imagining a conspiracy which did not exist, in order to justify his Purely racialistic and entirely irrational discriminatory prejudice and hatred of the Jews as a whole. Of course there was some truth in their allegations, but they maintained, through the kaffir media systems, that this was the whole truth, when in fact large vistas of the truth had been omitted from the picture which had been prepared for the general public. This campaign, designed to persuade the people of the west and of the east that there was no truth whatsoever in Hitler's statements about the activities of the free masons, and that all actions which he had encouraged to curtail his allegedly madly imagined state of affairs were crimes which ought to be punished, culminated in the Nuremberg trials, one of history's most carefully contrived judicial pantomimes.

Naturally the media coverage portrayed these trials as one of the major landmarks in the history of human rights and impartial legal process. The view was expressed that the accused were fortunate even to get a trial, let alone a fair one, since less impartial victors may have summarily executed them in angry revenge. This media cover up picture of the Nuremberg trials continues to be sustained today, as it has been since the trials first took place. It needs but a brief glance at the record of these trials to discover that they had been virtually decided before they began, and that they were designed to inflict as much torment on the accused as possible, before they were finally disposed of.

The records of the Nuremberg trials, for those who care to go beyond the trite media picture of dastardly criminals being brought to justice by the just, provide a clear example of the extent to which the kaffir legal and kaffir medical systems can be employed to eliminate opposition.

Unlike Pound, whose political opinions had received hardly any publicity or coverage in the kaffir media system, the German propaganda machine had aired Hitler's views to such an extent that it was impossible to pretend that they did not exist. Whereas Pound's views had been contained by keeping him silenced, Hitler's views had to be rendered ineffective and made to look ridiculous by distorting them through exaggeration, and thereby discrediting them. This could only be achieved by presenting Hitler and his immediate followers as violent and inhuman psychopaths who, blinded by ignorance and racialist hatred, had terrorised the German people into not only attempting to eliminate all the Jews in Europe, but also fighting a war which they did not wish to fight in order to achieve that object. The means by which this impression was created were the Nuremberg trials. In the name of international law, which is otherwise known as the game of international expediency, and of justice, their words and actions were accordingly manipulated and arranged, so as to create the desired picture, which was then spread abroad by the free masonic controlled kaffir media system.

It was imperative that the accused should be found fit to stand trial, even though they were subsequently to be presented to the world as mentally deranged beings, who could hardly be described as humans. Clearly if any of them could successfully plead that they were unfit for trial then the impact and force of the picture which was to be presented to the public would be thereby diminished. Accordingly the appropriate free masonic medical experts were selected to adjudge the accused as being normal enough to stand trial, and it comes as no surprise to learn that this was the conclusion to which they all came. The only way to avoid standing trial was by committing suicide, a course of action which only a very limited number of the accused chose to adopt.

As in the case of Pound, the accused were kept in solitary confinement and in unsavoury conditions, albeit not out in the open, in order to soften them up for the impending judicial proceedings. It was during this period of solitary confinement, which lasted several months, that the accused were subjected to the famous Rorschach tests, the results and interpretations of which were subsequently used to great effect in the post trial free masonic propaganda campaign against the followers of Hitler. The tests were initially begun by an English psychiatrist, who some years later was to commit suicide on New Year's Eve by swallowing one of the cyanide capsules which had been found on Goering after his own suicide. Allah says in Qur'an that the one who does not follow the way of the prophets is self destroyed. This psychiatrist was not considered ideally suited for the leading psychiatrist role in the Nuremberg stage production, and was accordingly replaced by a more expert American free masonic expert early on in the show. It was this man who conducted the Rorschach tests on the accused and subsequently wrote volumes on his so called expert findings.

The basis of the Rorschach tests is to present the so called patient with a series of large symmetrical ink blots, each differing in shape and colour. The patient gives a verbal reaction to each blot as it is shown, stating what he or she sees in it. The medical so called expert then interprets the patient's reactions, on the understanding that what the patient has seen in the blot is in fact a reflection of the patient's own reality. It comes as no surprise to learn that the reactions of the accused to the Rorschach tests were interpreted so as to give kaffir medical expert backed credibility to the popular image which was being created, of the Nazis being depicted as dangerous psychopathic sub human beasts.

The underlying assumption behind these tests, that is that the Rorschach tests are a valid means of measuring what is normal and abnormal and what is sane and insane, is a fallacious one, not only because, as we have already seen, the kaffir conceptions of what is normal and what is sane are not connected to the true nature of existence, but in fact cover it up, but also because the methodology used is faulty. What the Rorschach method fails to make adequate provision for is the psychological make up of the medical expert who carries out the tests. Since there is truth in the assumption that the patient does see his or her own reflection in what is in front of him or her, it follows that this is also true for the medical expert, and that therefore the medical expert's reactions to the responses of the patient to the Rorschach test provide in themselves a further secondary Rorschach type response, so that any evaluation of the patient's response by the medical expert is in reality an evaluation by the expert of his or her own self.

The medical experts' interpretation of the Nuremberg accused's responses was in itself a reflection of the experts' own inner reality, just as much as the accused's reaction to the blots was initially a reflection of the accused's own inner reality. The description which the kaffir medical experts attributed to the accused in fact fitted themselves, just as the opinions which the kaffir medical experts had reached as regards Pound's sanity were in fact descriptions of the state of their own sanity.

This is one aspect of the underlying unity of existence of which the kaffir expert is unaware: that the patients a doctor has, reflect his or her reality, and that the persons who come before a judge, reflect his or her reality. This is why different doctors have different patients, and different judges have different people to deal with. As far as the Nuremberg trials were concerned, there was no difference between the accusers and the accused, and no difference between the judges and the judged and, what is more and contrary to established kaffir legal practice, the accusers and the judges were one and the same.

The idea that the kaffir expert is somehow a detached observer of life, is one of the hall marks of the kaffir view of existence. He or she thinks that because of his or her special knowledge, or rather superior ability in amassing and juggling with information, he or she is capable of forming a detached and objective view of reality in which he or she is neither directly nor indirectly implicated. The truth is that there is no split in existence. There is only One Reality. No one is separate from the rest of existence even if they imagine that to be the case. The truth is that everyone in creation only sees what is in their own heart. Whatever is in your heart appears before you in creation. Whatever you see in creation is a reflection of your self. All you ever get back from the world is the echo of your own voice.

It follows from what has just been said that the only real doctors are the awliya of Allah, that is the friends of Allah, who have been given the idhn, that is the authority, to cure the hidden illnesses of the heart and the self by Allah, and to lead people to knowledge and gnosis of Allah by Allah. The awliya of Allah who teach with idhn are the only doctors in the world who see things as they are, which is to say as they are not, with a direct seeing. The kaffir medical expert gives reality to what he imagines to be real but which in fact is illusory. The awliya of Allah give reality to the Real, Allah. It follows that the awliya who teach with idhn cannot lie. Whoever comes into their presence receives a true reflection of his or her own self, and at the same time benefits from, and is transformed by, the light of Allah which is their light. Since all this happens by Allah, and since the awliya know this, they are unable to charge money for what they do. This is the sign of the rightly guided man of Allah, that he is rightly guided by Allah, and that he does not ask for money, the complete antithesis of the kaffir medical expert. For the same reasons the awliya of Allah are the people who are best equipped to judge between people, when a judge is needed, because their furqan, that is their ability to discriminate between what is just and what is unjust, is from Qur'an and by Allah. Since they are the ones who have most knowledge of Allah, it follows that they have most knowledge of all that comes from Allah, and are therefore in the best position to decide matters. Since their hearts have been purified, they see with a clear seeing. Since they have great fear of Allah, it is not possible for them to be motivated by self interest or personal greed, since they know this would take them to the Fire. Further, since their self has been obliterated in Allah it follows that there is no self to be interested in, or rather they see that the whole of existence is their self, so that personal greed is an impossibility. The awliya of Allah are the complete antithesis of the kaffir legal experts, who are not in a position to judge anything because they do not see anything as it is.

The Charter which was drawn up principally by the American and English free masonic legal experts, and which defined how the Nuremberg trials were to be conducted, was framed in such a manner that it ensured that the desired end result of the trials would be achieved with ease. The official legal definitions of what was to constitute a crime, and the ways in which the commission of that crime was to be capable of being proved, were so wide and so favoured the prosecution lawyers, that even a child could have convicted the accused of the crimes with which they were charged. It must be emphasized that the accused were not tried in accordance with the rules and laws of an existing kaffir legal system, since this would have made the task of convicting them all far more difficult, and much more time consuming and expensive. In effect the free masonic legal experts created a legal system just for the purpose of the Nuremberg trials, with its own special rules of procedure and evidence, and with its own special definitions of the crimes with which the accused were charged. The manner in which the Nuremberg trials were conducted would have been easily proved to be what existing kaffir legal systems would have defined as a gross irregularity in the conduct of those trials, and accordingly the accused would all have had to be acquitted and their convictions quashed, had they been given the right of appeal to, for example, the English Court of Appeal or the House of Lords. It was in order to escape this possibility that a separate self contained legal system, without any rights of appeal, was created for the purposes of the Nuremberg trials.

There were four major crimes which most of the accused were charged with committing. Their definitions were so vague and so all embracing that a great many acts of war, which are inevitably committed by all concerned on both sides during the course of war, because that is the nature of war, could be shown to come within the ambit of those definitions, whenever it was convenient or expedient so to do. The four major crimes were Crimes against Humanity, War Crimes, Crimes against Peace, and Conspiracy to commit these crimes. It should be pointed out that since it was the free masons who had engineered the war in the first place, it follows that they were just as what the kaffir calls guilty of these crimes as the accused, if not more so.

The Charter also stated that it was a crime to belong to a criminal organisation. The Charter defined nearly all the organs of government and administration, and the armed forces of Germany, and its official and secret police forces and intelligence agencies, as being criminal organisations. Naturally these counterparts on the side of the Allies were not regarded as criminal organisations, despite the fact that they had been operated in basically the same way, and used basically the same methods, as the Germans throughout the war, for there is really no difference between one kaffir and another, whether they be English, American, Russian or German. Membership of one of these criminal organisations was defined as being prima facie evidence of the fact that the person concerned belonged to the Conspiracy to commit the other major crimes defined by the Charter. Since all the accused, and indeed more than half of the population of Germany, belonged to at least one of the bodies which were defined as being criminal organisations, it followed that they were all implicated in the Conspiracy to commit the other major crimes before the trials had even begun. All that had to be shown, once the trials had started, for the accused to be found guilty of the Conspiracy charge, was membership of one of what had been defined as criminal organisations. In effect the free masons were accusing the German leaders of the very conspiracy which they themselves were involved in, and which Hitler had unsuccessfully tried to expose and destroy. By boldly turning the tables in this way, the free masons hoped to provide an effective smoke screen to cover up and obscure the true nature of their own activities. It would seem that their hopes were fulfilled, for even at the time of writing this, the wind still has not blown that smoke screen away.

The fact that the Charter defined nearly all the national kaffir institutions in Germany as being criminal for the purpose of the trials, as well as ensuring that the accused would be automatically found guilty of the Conspiracy charge, not only effectively allowed the free masons to charge whoever they wished to charge, but also indirectly ensured that there would be very few witnesses for the defence indeed. Whilst the judicial machinery for the trials was being prepared, large quantities of leaflets were distributed amongst the German people, requesting members of what had been defined as criminal organisations to give themselves up, and asking any potential witnesses in the impending proceedings to step forward and identify themselves. Any member of one of the so called called criminal organisations who gave him or her self up could then be charged, if the prosecution thought it necessary, and all without any of the bother and expense of having to go out and find them. Any potential witness who was foolish enough to identify him or her self was often immediately arrested and charged with belonging to one of the criminal organisations. If the person in question agreed to act as a prosecution witness, and not as a defence witness, then it could be arranged that the charges against him or her would be dropped. If it was not possible to eliminate a potential defence witness in this way, he or she was often successfully deterred and discouraged from giving evidence by being beaten up. The few defence witnesses who survived this screening process were, like the accused, kept imprisoned in solitary confinement in order to break them down and weaken their morale. No real distinction was ever made between the accused and the few defence witnesses who were able to give evidence at the trial. By the time the trials were under way their value as witnesses, and the weight of their testimony, had been so effectively eroded and undermined by the treatment which they had received, that really their only function was to help create the impression that the accused were receiving a fair trial.

This technique of inducing people to give themselves up voluntarily, and of persuading them to incriminate their colleagues in order to save their own skins, is strongly reminiscent of the techniques used by the Spanish Inquisition to achieve exactly the same objects, the only difference between them being that the Spanish Inquisitors were after Jews, Unitarian Christians and Muslims, whilst the Nuremberg prosecutors were after fellow kaffirs. It may well be that the Nuremberg prosecutors were aware of and followed the example of the Spanish Inquisition, since the Spanish Inquisitors were then what the free masons of today are.

The Nuremberg prosecutors, who in open disregard of the kaffir doctrine of the separation of powers legislative, administrative and judicial, were also the legislators of the Charter and the judges of the accused, based their case largely on documentary evidence. The advantage of this approach was, and is, that you cannot cross examine a piece of paper as to the truth of its contents, and a verbal denial alone of the truth of those contents or of a particular interpretation of or construction which has been placed upon those contents, is hardly ever sufficient to rebut the evidence apparently contained in the document in question, especially if the judge is in fact already entirely in agreement with the prosecution case. The rules relating to documentary evidence which usually apply to judicial proceedings in the kaffir courts of the west, and which give at least a limited guarantee of the possibility of being able to establish whether or not what is stated in the document is accurate, were for the purposes of the Nuremberg trials waived completely. This meant that the Nuremberg prosecutors could conduct their case in a manner which normally, even by kaffir standards of normality, would have been condemned and brought to a halt for being both biased and oppressive, and contrary to the laws of what the kaffir legal systems define as natural justice and international law. Indeed it was even openly argued that since the accused's actions were breaches of international law, therefore they could not expect to enjoy the protection of international law, let alone to be tried in accordance with it.

Basically the prosecution were allowed to adduce whatever document they wanted to in evidence even if it was second or third hand hearsay, let alone first hand hearsay, and even if the document was not an original but a copy. This meant that forged documents could also be introduced into the prosecution evidence without being challenged by the defence. Even if a document was challenged as being of suspect origin, naturally there was a sworn affidavit available by a sufficiently high ranking free masonic legal expert, which stated that all documents were original documents and had been verified as such by whoever had found them. The Nuremberg prosecutors were given carte blanche by virtue of Articles 18 and 19 of the Charter. Under Article 18 of the Charter the Tribunal was to confine the trial to an expeditious hearing, and to take strict measures to prevent any action which would cause unreasonable delay, and to rule out irrelevant issues and statements of any kind whatsoever. Article 19 of the Charter stated that the Tribunal should not be bound by technical rules of evidence, and that it should adopt and apply to the greatest possible extent expeditious and non technical procedure, and that it should admit any evidence which it deemed to have probative value.

Any one who cares to read the record of the Nuremberg trials will see how time and again the Tribunal used Article 18 to silence the Defence, and allowed the Prosecution to adduce whatever so called evidence they wished under and by virtue of Article 19. Of course the Charter also provided, by virtue of Article 3, that any attempt to question the validity of the Tribunal's jurisdiction, or its right to try the accused in the first place, should be dismissed without further ado.

The Nuremberg prosecutors were not only able to adduce whatever piece of paper they wanted in evidence, but also often did so without having served copies of these documents on the defence prior to their

71

being produced. Furthermore it sometimes happened that when an incriminating document's contents were worded in a language other than German, no translation was provided for the defence lawyers. Whenever this happened it meant that they were forced to rely solely on the simultaneous translation service provided by IBM, which translated whatever was being said at the time into English, French, Russian and German, usually about a sentence behind and often inaccurately. In effect this meant that the defence lawyers did not know what case they had to meet until the very last moment, which gave them very little time to prepare the defence. Furthermore the defence lawyers were not permitted to converse with the accused in the court room. They could only communicate by written note. This again limited what the defence lawyer could do when an unexpected point was raised by the prosecution, since written communication was so much slower than the whispered word, when it came to trying to ascertain what the accused's response was to the point in question.

The Tribunal also permitted the prosecution to adduce in evidence sworn affidavits of alleged prosecution witnesses who were, so it was said, unable to attend. This meant that that the defence lawyers were unable to test the truth of the contents of these affidavits by cross examining the people who had made them in the witness box, and to ask the questions which had purposely not been asked by the prosecutor who had prepared the affidavits. The Tribunal permitted the production of these affidavits under Article 19, blandly stating that it would take into account the fact that such statements did not have as much probative value as they would have had if the person making them had been in the witness box and available for cross examination, and that accordingly not so much weight would be attached to them. The truth of the matter is that the nature of the evidence was such that, although to a layman it must have seemed as though it was all being presented in accordance with sound judicial precept and established legal practice, in fact it was not only heavily biased, but also the Tribunal could put whatever interpretation and whatever weight they wished on it. Indeed the conclusions they were to draw had already been reached long before any of the evidence was formally presented for their consideration.

By basing their case on documentary evidence, and by adducing that evidence in the manner in which they were permitted to adduce it, the prosecution lawyers were able to say what they wanted without fear of being effectively challenged by the defence lawyers, and without having to rely on live witnesses, who might possibly have come out with evidence which was favourable to the accused. The prosecution lawyers were also helped by the fact that the accused had only been permitted to choose their defence lawyers from a list of lawyers which had been prepared by the prosecutors, who no doubt had been sure to ensure that only free masons, or lawyers who would not put up too much of a fight or ask too many awkward questions, or lawyers who were unfamiliar with the mainly American and English judicial techniques and procedures which were being employed by the prosecutors, were included on that list. In effect any lawyer who might possibly be aware of what the free masons were up to, and who would be prepared to oppose and expose their activities, was excluded from that list of eligible defence lawyers, and accordingly prevented from representing the accused. Furthermore although the Charter gave the accused the right of conducting their own defence if they so wished, they were in fact deterred and prevented from exercising that right. This meant not only that they were prevented from saying more than was minimally necessary during the course of the proceedings, but also that they were represented by tame lawyers, since any lawyer worth his salt would have objected far more strongly about the manner in which, and the basis on which, the proceedings were being conducted than the defence lawyers who were chosen to represent the accused actually did.

The other advantage of basing the prosecution case on documentary evidence was this: At the end of the war the American and English command had set up special documentation centres, and as their forces advanced into Germany, they collected and transported all the official documents which they found to these centres. Literally hundreds of tons of documents were collected at these centres. The highly trained personnel at these centres subsequently sifted through the considerable tonnage of these documents, and retained all those which helped to support the prosecution case. Those sections of the written word or the filmed event which did not help the prosecution case were erased or cut, when and wherever possible. Any documents or films which might establish the so called innocence of the accused, or assist their defence lawyers in their attempts to exonerate the accused, were retained and either destroyed or at least certainly not disclosed to the other side. As it happened there were some documents amongst the many thousands which were made available to the Nuremberg prosecutors, which had passed unnoticed through the documentation centre screening process, and which turned out to be favourable to the defence case. As soon as this fact was appreciated, the documents in question suddenly disappeared from the safe in which all the documents which were to be adduced in evidence were kept in safe keeping. The prosecution thus had access to and control over all the documents which they wished to adduce in evidence, whilst the defence had virtually no access to any documents at all, except the useless documents which the prosecutors allowed them to have.

The Nuremberg prosecutors could produce whatever document they wanted, whenever they wanted, without having warned the defence of their intention so to do, with the exception that is of the less important and the less incriminating documents, and certainly without having permitted the defence to have a copy of the document in question before it was actually produced to the court. As it was, it quite often happened that when documents were suddenly produced in this manner, there was no copy available for the defence lawyer who needed it, and if several defence lawyers each needed a copy of a certain document, it often happened that if there were copies available, they were insufficient in number so that they had to be shared. These tactics ensured that the defence lawyers, ill equipped as they were, were never in a position to meet the case which was being levelled at the people whom they represented. At best often all that could be mustered was a flat and empty denial of whatever was being alleged, a denial which was easily muffled and silenced by the mountains of paper ammunition which was at the disposal of the prosecution.

It is clear that many of the accused in the Nuremberg trials had been responsible either directly or indirectly for the deaths of other people during the war. If they had been charged with murder, or attempted murder, or conspiracy to commit murder, and tried in an ordinary kaffir court of law in accordance with existing kaffir legal principles and procedures, they probably would have been found guilty on at least one of those counts. However it must be remembered that the purpose of the Nuremberg trials was not merely to find the principal followers of Hitler guilty of capital offences so that they could be legally eliminated. The main purpose of the Nuremberg trials was to create a sufficiently grandiose yet illusory diversion in order to direct the general public's attention away from the activities of the free masons, and cause them to lay the causes of the second kaffir world war fairly, or rather unfairly, and squarely at the door of the German people.

The outcome of the Nuremberg trials was a foregone conclusion. What is interesting is the extent to which the free masons were prepared to go in order firstly to create the illusion of a fair trial, conducted in accordance with due judicial process, secondly to arrange the presentation of evidence in such a way that a completely false yet convincing picture of how the war was started and what the Germans did in it was made to emerge, and thirdly to make sure this false yet convincing picture was subsequently spread across the face of the earth and accepted by the great majority of those who either saw or heard about it.

The free masons, like the magicians of Pharaoh, are today's masters of illusion. They mesmerise people with illusions, so as to be able to control and manipulate them, and the Nuremberg trials illusion was perhaps one of their greatest feats of illusion, masking a masterly exercise in manipulation control, thanks to the combined efforts of the medical and legal kaffir experts, and ensuring not only that the important followers of Hitler were both utterly discredited and eliminated in the process, but also that the general public of the world were taken in by that illusion.

The publicity which this exercise in mass manipulation received and needed was of course provided by the free masonic controlled media systems, which were in a position to provide the right pictures and exerpts from speeches and loaded commentaries needed to create the desired impression of an impressive and just judicial assembly who were trying, with all the apparent detachment and impartiality in the world, a motley and inhuman group of psychopathic desperadoes, who really did not even deserve the fair trial which they appeared to be getting, in the first place. Clearly the part played by the media systems of the kaffirs was and continues to be very significant. Creating the desired picture was relatively child's play. The real challenge was to make sure that this picture subsequently found its way into the recesses of the majority of the general public's minds. The fact that it did, and has, indicates not only the extreme efficiency of the free masons, but also the high degree of control which they exercise over a great many people through their media systems. Big brother may not have been watching you, but he has certainly been programming and conditioning you.

In reality there was little or no difference between the people who tried the accused in the Nuremberg trials and the accused who were tried. In reality the second kaffir world war was no more or less than a power struggle between opposing pyrammidical kaffir power systems.

Allah says in Qur'an that the kaffirs appear to be one body, but in fact they are divided against each other. The prophet Muhammad, may the blessings and peace of Allah be on him, said that kufr is one system. Thus in effect the second kaffir world war was one unified event involving one system, that is the kaffir system, that is the Dajjal system, involved in destroying itself. Allah says in Qur'an that a people who do not follow the way of the prophets are self destroyed, that is they destroy themselves and each other.

The success of the Nuremberg trials, as far as the free masons were and are concerned, can be measured by the fact that if you say to anyone in the street today, that is anyone who has been exposed to the usual kaffir educational and kaffir media kaffir conditioning process, the one word Hitler, or Nazi, or Nuremberg, then the magical figure and phrase of six million Jews murdered in the concentration camps will probably spring to his or her lips, or at least flash across his or her mind, even though it was never actually established during the Nuremberg trials, or subsequently, that anything like that number of Jews were killed in this way, and by the methods purported to have been used by those who controlled the concentration camps. When the figure of six million was being decided on by the free masons who were most concerned with publicity, Weitzmann, who is one of the public figure head founders of the Zionist movement, is reputed to have supported the six million mark, by saying that the people will not believe a little lie, but they will believe a big one. Further it should be remembered that the phrase, concentration camp, is now a very emotionally loaded term, due to the way it has been used by the free masonic media systems. These camps were basically prisoner of war camps. Prisoner of war camps were popularised by the British as they built up the British Empire, and then tried to keep it, but in fact there have always been prisoner of war camps as long as there have been wars in which people have been taken prisoner in large numbers.

The reality of the second kaffir world war is that the actions of nearly all the people concerned in it, on both sides, at some time or other came within the ambit of one or other of the crimes as defined by the sweeping terms of the Nuremberg Charter, which in effect made it a crime to plan a war and fight it in the way that kaffir wars are usually fought.

Kaffir wars are fought indiscriminately, whereas jihad, that is a fight in the way of Allah by those who trust in Allah, is fought on the basis that you may only fight in self defence, and that you may not kill anyone who says the shahada, that is anyone who affirms that there is no god only Allah and that Muhammad is the messenger of Allah, and that you must not kill in anger, since that will take you to the Fire, and that you may not pillage and rape if Allah gives you victory, and finally that if you die in the jihad, then you will die directly witnessing Allah and go straight to the Garden. The kaffir fights in complete ignorance of what lies on the other side of death, and is therefore careless in whom he or she kills, and what he or she does. The muslim fights with intense awareness of what lies on the other side of death, fearful in the knowledge that fighting for the wrong reason, or killing the wrong person, can result in him or her ending up in the Fire, and accordingly the muslim is very careful in whom he or she kills and in what he or she does.

It is interesting to note that the kaffir definitions of the major crimes embodied in the Charter did not take the next world into consideration at all. If one views the actions of both sides from the limited perspective of the terms of the Charter then everyone who fought in the war was guilty of those crimes, especially the free masons who not only master minded the war but also drew up the Charter. The victors however were in a position to shut their eyes to this fact, whilst the vanquished were prevented from voicing it publicly.

It is interesting to note that in the relatively minor wars which the free masons have arranged since the end of the second kaffir world war, the actions of notably the American and English forces, which have borne an evident and marked resemblance to those of the German forces in the last war, have not been punished at the hands of military tribunals, but rather praised as being the valiant attempts of those who were prepared to sacrifice their lives for their country, in the name of peace, freedom and justice, in the war against the communists, or the terrorists, or the fanatics, or whoever the free masonic controlled media has depicted as being the enemy.

Basically the kaffir media systems can depict whoever they want as being the enemy. This is done by using highly emotive vocabulary, such as the words communists, terrorists, fanatics, whose very mention conjures up an immediate emotional response in any listener who has been adequately conditioned by the kaffir educational and media systems. This emotional response takes the form of immediate rejection and condemnation of whoever has been described by these key kaffir definitions, so that the person in whom the response arises is totally incapable of seeing who the people so described really are, and of examining what they are really saying. Furthermore it is impossible for the person who relies on the kaffir media version of events ever to find out what the truth of the matter really is, since all that he or she has to go on is what he or she is presented with, and this, as we have seen from the examples of Ezra Pund and the Nuremberg trials, is often very far from the truth. The free masonic controlled kaffir media systems can basically create any illusion they wish, and as long as the validity of their techniques remains unchallenged, get away with it.

The term, fanatic, is usually reserved for the muslims; the term communist, is usually reserved for the non muslims who wish to take over control of the kaffir system from its present masters; and the term, terrorist, is usually reserved for the people in either of these two groups who are prepared to act rather than talk. The difference between the muslims and what the kaffir calls the capitalists, is the same as the difference between the muslims and what the kaffir calls the communists. The muslims accept Allah and His messengers, whilst the capitalists and the communists reject Allah and his messengers.

In reality there is no difference between the capitalists and the communists. Capitalism and communism are the same. The capitalists and the communists are kaffirs. They appear to be divided against each other, but they are the same body. Kufr is one system. The capitalists and the communists both base their societies on identical interlinking pyrammidical systems structures. They share the same kaffir view of existence. They fight for the same things and worship the same idols. Their leaders follow the same behavioural life pattern. They both use kaffir ideologies, and although they employ a different vocabulary that is a different term of reference to describe their actions and what they are doing, they in fact both affirm and sustain the kaffir producer consumer process, which can only operate as it does today if the many are enslaved by that process for the benefit of the few. Although they pretend to be at war with each other, and to be separated by their imaginary iron curtain, they in fact trade with each other and sustain each other's economies. They both use exactly the same methods and manipulation techniques to condition their people to accept the goals of the consumer producer process, and to be content with its apparent rewards, despite and in spite of the reality of the human situation which is that only the rememberance of Allah stills the heart. As we have already seen, this conditioning is only possible where the educational and media institutions and systems are in the control of the few, that is the kaffir ruling elite, so as to enable them to create the illusion not only that their legal system is what they call just, not only that their medical system is what they call advanced, not only that their educational system provides what they call knowledge, but also that he consumer producer process is what man was created for, and that here is no viable alternative way of life to it.

Indeed it is one of the favourite arguments of the kaffir politician to ay, whenever the kaffir system, that is the Dajjal system, is criticised, hat it may not be perfect but at least it is better than anarchy. The vord, anarchy, is another key emotional term in the kaffir media ystem vocabulary. The emotional response which it is desired to rigger off in the listener is a vision of absolute chaos, which with any uck will reach apocalyptic proportions if the listener has a good magination backed up by the typical kaffir's fear of creation and overty, a fear which always exists in an ignorant person who does not now how existence works. This apparent lack of choice, which ypifies the either you accept society as it is or else there will be anarchy pproach to life, is another example of the persuasive power which the affir media system exercises over the people whom it helps to ondition.

Indeed it is one of the characteristics of the kaffir system, that is the Dajjal system, that as long as a person accepts his or her conditioning nd the kaffir definitions of the nature of existence, it is impossible to nvisage or imagine any other alternative to that system, so strong is he influence of that conditioning. This is one of the reasons why any drug which is capable of lifting a person's consciousness free of that onditioning, and altering that perception of existence, is defined as eing illegal by most kaffir legal systems. The only drugs which are ermitted in a kaffir state are those which will mildly stimulate or nildly tranquillise. This does not mean that drugs are necessary to lter the consciousness. The way of the prophet Muhammad wakes ou up to the true nature of existence in a way which nothing else can, endering all drugs obsolete.

It is only those who have seen the kaffir system, that is the Dajjal ystem, for what it is, and who have rejected it, who are able to begin to ppreciate the only viable alternative to the kaffir system that is the Dajjal system, which is Islam. The only way to really appreciate what he way of Islam is, is to follow that way, for to read about the journey, r to examine the map, is not the same as actually making the journey. The one who sets out on this journey progressively tastes the deep anity which springs from the knowledge of how existence works, and he peace and certainty which this knowledge brings.

Allah says in Qur'an: "I did not create man and jinn except to vorship Me." To embody the guidance contained in the Qur'an, as xemplified by the prophet Muhammad and the first muslim

community of Madina al Munawarra, is to worship Allah in ever
moment. Many people in the west who have become disenchante
with the kaffir system, that is the Dajjal system, no matter how high u
in one of its hierarchical sub systems they may be or may have been
are beginning to find out the truth of these words for themselves. Man
people in the east who were beguiled by the surface attractions of th
illusory rewards of the producer consumer system, which had bee
successfully introduced into their countries by the colonisers, are now
beginning to rediscover the living life transaction of Islam fo
themselves. The resurgence of Islam in these times, which wa
predicted by the prophet Muhammad, and which is already very muc
in evidence despite the attempts of the kaffir media systems to disguis
and discredit it, cannot be compared to the rise of Hitler's movement
and his attempts to replace one kaffir power structure by another kaffi
power structure. Hitler and his followers were part of the phenomeno
of Dajjal as a world wide social and cultural phenomenon and Dajjal a
an unseen force. The present resurgence of Islam is the sign that th
present dominant kaffir culture is about to be replaced and eclipsed b
another way of life, which is its complete antithesis and entirel
different to it, that is the prophetic way of life.

It follows that all the kaffir governments which at the time of writin
control nearly all of the muslim countries in the name of Islam, but i
accordance with kaffir modes of manipulation control, will inevitabl
be replaced by real muslims who govern in accordance with what is i
Qur'an. These so called islamic kaffir governments are part of th
Dajjal system. The people who control them are identified in th
Hadith as being people whose hearts will be devoid of Qur'an, becaus
it will not be able to descend beyond their throats. Their appearanc
on the face of the earth is one of the signs of the end of the world. Th
prophet Muhammad said that they would go out of Islam faster than a
arrow leaves the bow, and that they would be the worst people on th
face of the earth. The destination of the munafiqoon, that is the peopl
who say that they are muslim when in reality they are not, is th
deepest part of the Fire.

The present resurgence of Islam is the necessary preliminary prior t
the appearance of the Mahdi, just as the recent ascendance in th
influence of the kaffir system that is the Dajjal system, throughout th
world, is the necessary preliminary prior to the appearance of Dajja
the individual.

The examples provided by the treatment of Ezra Pound and the Nuremberg so called war criminals are dramatic ones. They demonstrate the extreme limits to which the people who control the kaffir system that is the Dajjal system are prepared to go in order to ensure the continued survival of their control over that system. They are by no means however the only examples. One only has to observe what is going on around one, to recognize how the Dajjal system operates and what its free masonic controlling elite are up to. The machinations of this system in all its various activities in all spheres of life, and the actions of its controlling elite, are everywhere in evidence for the one who looks, no matter how hard and cunningly that elite attempts to hide and disguise those activities and actions. The actions and activities are always manifest, but it is the meaning of those actions and activities which is so often obscured by the kaffir educational and media smoke screen and conditioning techniques. By presenting a fragmented view of existence these systems prevent people from adding two and two together, and arriving at an overall understanding of what is going on. The people who split existence, or rather create that illusion since in Reality existence can not be split because there is only Allah, are described in Qur'an as the fasiqoon, that is the people who divide.

Division characterises the actions and activities of the kaffir, and division is the inevitable result of the way in which the kaffir system, that is the Dajjal system, operates. This is why cancer is a physiological illness of this age. This is why schizophrenia and autism are psychological illnesses of this age. This is why nationalism and modern tribal warfare are social illnesses of this age. Whether within the individual, or in the family group, or in kaffir society as a whole, we see division, the result of the way of life of the fasiqoon, that is the people who operate and uphold the kaffir system, that is the Dajjal system.

Clearly there are many people who suffer from the manner in which the Dajjal system operates and who are enslaved by it, but who do not realise what the cause of that suffering is nor realise the nature of the prison they are in. As a result of their conditioning they continue to play an active and often important part in the running of the very system which unbeknown to them is the cause of their pain and the invisible walls of their prison. Drinking alcohol or taking drugs is no cure, rather these activities are part of the disease. It is the actual existential pattern of behaviour, together with the mental outlook that

81

goes with it, which is the disease, simply because they are not in harmony with the true nature of existence, and accordingly that imbalance manifests in illness whether physiological, psychological, social or political.

The influence and overall control of the kaffir system, that is the Dajjal system, are so widespread and insidiously present in all aspects of people's lives today, that the majority of people are unaware of what confronts them. The Dajjal system is as much a part of their lives as the air around them, which they breathe and depend on without knowing it. The free masonic control which is exercised over them is so much a part of their every day lives, it is so close up to them, that they do not see it, just as they do not see that their being is from Allah, and that they are entirely dependant on Allah for their every heart beat. The truth of things is a blur in the corner of their eye. They have been born into the Dajjal system, and brought up to accept that this is the way life is. They have been educated in the Dajjal system's ways and continually misled by the media to affirm it, even after their formal education has been completed. Even when someone is aware that not all is well, he or she is often not able to say why or what. A person may glimpse an instance of blatant kaffir media manipulation, or witness a particular example of the injustice of the kaffir legal system at work, or admit deep down that he or she has learnt nothing of real value in the official curriculum of kaffir school or university, and yet be unable to form a clear picture of the kaffir system, that is the Dajjal system, or to pull free from the influence of the kaffir producer consumer process in which he or she is trapped.

In reality every atom is in its place and everything which appears to take place in existence is a part of one unified event. In Reality that one unified event does not exist. There is only Allah. Allah is the Inwardly Hidden and the Outwardly Manifest. Allah is the First before time began and the Last after time ceased. Wherever you look there is the face of Allah. Everything is passing away except the face of Allah. Surely we come from Allah and to Allah we surely return. The difference between the kaffir way of life and the muslim way of life is that the kaffir way of life prevents you from seeing this, whilst the muslim way of life not only opens this knowledge up to you, but also enables you to live with it at peace and in tranquillity. The kaffir thinks that he or she exists, and is troubled, whilst the mumin knows that Allah exists, and is at peace.

The needs and demands of everyday life in a kaffir society, whether actual or merely media created, which because of the complex nature of the Dajjal system are themselves complex and in profusion, make it difficult for most people to stop and reflect, let alone to make the decision as a result of that reflection to abandon the kaffir way of life, to de-programme and de-condition, and to find out who they really are and what the true nature of existence really is. Indeed the influence of the Dajjal system is such that the person enslaved by it believes that the kaffir way of life is the only viable way of life, is not aware that he or she has been programmed and conditioned, and thinks that his or her kaffir view of existence is correct and unclouded. Even if, despite all this, that decision is reached, it is difficult to act on it existentially without coming up against the preventative and deterrent provisions of the kaffir legal system, which have been designed to prevent people straying too far from the limits of what the kaffir system that is the Dajjal system has defined as normal and legal. Furthermore there are strong social pressures from relations and friends who may be relatively content with the system as it is, and who will be correspondingly appalled at your decision to leave it, and therefore be prepared to do all that they can, whether by means of financial inducement, emotional blackmail or even physical force, to dissuade you from acting on your decision. For those who, despite all these contrary forces, still feel impelled to seek real knowledge and the balanced way of life which must necessarily accompany that search, many subsequently find that they are only prepared to go so far, either because they do not want all that there is to be wanted, or else because fear of being punished silenced or eliminated by the kaffir free masonic manipulation control system acts as a deterrent, and induces the would be searcher back into playing the kaffir producer consumer game.

Only those who fear Allah alone are free from fear of other than Allah, and accordingly are free from fear of the kaffir system, that is the Dajjal system, and its varied means of norm enforcement.

The people who only fear Allah alone are those who follow the way of the prophet Muhammad. Clearly those people who have not yet encountered the way of Islam, although they may have a misconceived idea of what it is, as a result of their kaffir educational and media programming, and who are at present caught up in the kaffir consumer producer process, will have fear of the powers that appear to be in the kaffir system, that is the Dajjal system, even though they have already inwardly rejected that system. Furthermore the existential panic and anxiety about provision and shelter, which inevitably arise in the heart of whoever does not know how existence works, reinforce the fear of the Dajjal system, and act as an added incentive to continue to act in accordance with the dictates of the consumer producer system, which promises to relieve that panic and anxiety by coming up with the goods. The deal is that if you play the consumer producer game, then you will be given the money to buy the goods which you have been conditioned to want. In fact this is a lie, since, as we have already noted, one of the ways of keeping people working in the kaffir producer consumer process is to pay them a sum which will not meet all their needs, so that firstly they have to continue to work to live, and secondly they have to continue to work to pay off the debts swelled by interest which they have been encouraged to incur by the various free masonic controlled kaffir finance systems. The nature of the Dajjal system is such that only the controlling elite are in a position to enjoy the rewards of the labours of all the others. Indeed it has to be this way, since there simply are not enough luxury items in existence for everyone in a kaffir society to enjoy them.

Even the people, who receive more than their fair share of the myriad goods which today's consumer producer system manufactures, do not find that their existential panic and anxiety have been quelled, and accordingly they only become lost in the endless search for the latest model and the ultimate thing, neither of which exist.

The fact that mere consumption is not the answer to anxiety about provision is true for two main reasons. Firstly this anxiety is the result of ignorance of how existence works, and accordingly will only begin to disappear when that ignorance is replaced by knowledge. Secondly the restlessness, which every man and woman feels deep in the heart, is no less than the longing for knowledge of Allah, and accordingly that longing and that restlessness can only be appeased by knowledge of Allah. Real knowledge of Allah only comes with rememberance of Allah, and accordingly it is only in the rememberance of Allah that the heart finds rest. It is only possible to remember Allah if you follow the way of the messengers who have been sent by Allah during the various ages of mankind. The messenger who was sent by Allah for the present age is the prophet Muhammad, and accordingly it is only by following his way that fear of existence and existential panic and anxiety about provision and shelter will disappear. The choice is yours right now.

Although the choice is clear, it is not easy to make for the one who has been conditioned by the Dajjal system, even if the person in question is in the process of rejecting that conditioning. The conditioning provided by the Dajjal system is insidiously strong. It creates in the mind of the individual the impression that the only way to dispel fear and anxiety is by taking the remedies offered by that system, that is to work and to play when you are well, and to do what the doctor tells you when you are ill, and above all not to try and change the status quo either inwardly or outwardly. In effect the one who has been conditioned by the Dajjal system is never really permitted to grow up, even though he or she is capable of having children and holding down an office job and driving a car. The one who has been conditioned by the Dajjal system is kept in awe of that system, in the same way that a young child is not only in awe of the parents but also thinks that they are the best parents in the world and know everything. Everyone who is not involved in seeking knowledge of Allah is a child, for it is only when you reach a certain age that you begin to wish to know the nature of existence. Some people never emotionally or intellectually reach that age. Some people simply do not have intellect, which in Qur'an is called aql, nor do they have what Qur'an calls lubb, that is a core, that is the access to the innermost secret of their being. There is no blame in this. Everyone can only be who they are. Allah has made some people kaffir and some people mumin. Allah has made some people ignorant and some people knowledgeable. Allah has made some people blind and some people seeing. They are not the same, but there is no blame. The mercy of Allah covers the whole of creation and pervades it in every respect. The kaffir does not see this whilst the mumin does.

Clearly there are those who are utterly blind, and there are those who are utterly seeing, and there are those who are somewhere in between blindness and sight. A distinction must therefore be drawn between the one who is quite content with the Dajjal system such as it is for what it is worth, and the one who cannot bear it and is only interested in following the way of Muhammad in all its rich simplicity, and the one who does not particularly like the Dajjal system but who has not yet encountered the way of Muhammad.

Allah says in Qur'an that people either follow the way of the prophets or they follow the way of their fathers. Clearly there are a great many people in the world today who have not had access to the living and vibrant life transaction of the prophet Muhammad, as it was lived by him and the first muslim community of Madina al Munawarra, and who accordingly have been following the way of their fathers, no matter how ignorant that way might be, simply because they do not know any better. These people cannot really be described as being kaffir, since a kaffir is one who has actually been presented with a clear exposition of what Islam is and what Allah requires of him or her, and who has then openly rejected what he or she has heard, and subsequently attempted to shut out all mention or manifestation of the way of Islam.

It also frequently happens that a person, because the self is poisoned with ignorance, at first rejects the way of Islam, because to a sick person what is sweet often tastes bitter and what is bitter often tastes sweet, but then in the ripeness of time accepts the way of Islam. Allah says in Qur'an that it is Allah who expands the heart to accept Islam, and Allah does as He wishes.

It follows that there are a great many people in the kaffir states of the world who, although they are at present trapped by the Dajjal system and caught up in the daily whirl of the consumer producer process, will, when Allah wishes it, and once they have encountered real muslims and experienced what Islam really is and means, themselves become muslim. Of course there will be those who utterly reject the way of Islam. Allah says of these people in Qur'an that their ears and eyes are veiled so that they cannot hear what a muslim says or see what a muslim does with any true understanding. Whether you talk to them or not, it is the same. They are blind, deaf and dumb, even though they appear to see, and hear, and speak. Allah guides whom He wishes, and Allah leads astray whom He wishes. Allah sends some to the Garden and He does not care, and Allah sends some to the Fire and He does not care. Allah has power over everything. There is no strength and no power except from Allah.

The present resurgence of Islam is a clear indication from Allah that the polarisation of the people of iman and the people of kufr on a world scale is under way. This polarisation is necessary before their respective leaders, the Mahdi for the muslims and Dajjal the individual for the kaffirs, can appear, and before the two opposites meet as they inevitably must, since anyone who is kaffir cannot help but attack any one who is muslim, and once the muslims are attacked, Allah has ordered them to fight back in self defence and to kill their aggressors, that is anyone who attacks them and refuses to say the shahada, that is to state that there is no god only Allah and that Muhammad is the messenger of Allah.

One way of measuring the level of ignorance in a kaffir society, and the corresponding fear of existence and anxiety about provision and shelter which arise out of that ignorance, which is the hall mark of the kaffir system, that is the Dajjal system, is to examine the extent to which people insure themselves and their goods against possible disaster and misfortune, even when they are not required to do so by kaffir law. The kaffir insurance system is totally unnecessary for the people who know how existence works, and who follow the prophetic life pattern which is its own insurance.

Since everyone meets the consequences of their actions both in this life and the next, it follows that the one who is unaware of what action is fruitful and what action is unfruitful often brings misfortune upon him or her self, solely because of the way he or she acts. Since the kaffir does not know this, he or she seeks to avoid the effects of the misfortune by insuring against it before it happens, rather than abandoning the course of action which is the real cause of the misfortune.

The way of Muhammad is the science of fruitful action. In Qur'an fruitful action is called halal, whilst unfruitful action is called haram. Although these words are sometimes translated respectively as meaning what is permitted and what is forbidden, their real meaning is to be found in the consequences of the actions which they describe. If this perspective is lost, it often happens that the conceptual framework, which the kaffir calls morality, is allowed to develop.

The moral mental attitude makes people forget where they are going. It works like this: To begin with there is the knowledge that what is halal is fruitful in this world and leads to the Garden in the next world, whilst what is haram is unfruitful in this world and leads to the Fire in the next world. This applies even to the food which you eat, because if you eat halal food your actions will be halal, and if you eat haram food your actions will be haram. Drinking wine or eating haram meat are not serious actions in themselves, but the actions which arise out of these actions often are. They lead not only to an imbalance in the body but also to an imbalance in actions, an imbalance which causes distress in this world and is experienced as the Fire in the next world. In the same way doing what is halal leads to balanced action which results in harmony in this world and is experienced as the Garden in the next world.

This perspective begins to be lost when it is said that halal means permitted and haram means forbidden, because often it is forgotten exactly why an action is permitted or forbidden. The original perspective is further clouded when a value judgement is placed on what is permitted and what is forbidden, that is when what is described as halal is called good, and when what is described as haram is called bad, again because it becomes easier to forget why it is good or why it is bad. If the overall perspective of the next world is lost, then people forget why something is really good or bad. Instead they begin to form fixed ideas of what is good and what is bad. Then, if they forget that Allah looks at the intention behind the action and not the action itself, they begin to be less critical of their own actions, since they no longer fear the Fire or hope for the Garden, and become more critical of other's actions. They begin to judge the outward actions of others, even though unaware of what the intention behind those actions might be, in accordance with their ideas of what is good and what is bad.

Once people forget about the Fire and the Garden, and indeed cease to know that the next world exists, they then begin to call what is expedient good and what is not expedient bad. In effect their idea of what is good and what is bad is no longer connected to the true realities of life, but rather is attached to what they give reality. Once this stage has been reached, you have what the kaffir calls morality, that is a complex web of do's and don't's which are given spurious validity by emotional value judgements, which often have no relation to the true nature of existence, and which accordingly only cause the one who has this moral mental attitude to forget where he or she is going, that is to Allah, via the Fire or the Garden.

Anyone who becomes aware of the hypocrisy which inevitably arises out of the kaffir morality usually then rejects it. Once they have rejected it they have no frame of reference to use when dealing with situations which require judgement, other than what they have learned from experience, that is they have a limited knowledge of what is halal and haram, which they have arrived at by trial and error, and the significance of which they do not realise, because they do not link this limited knowledge of what is halal and what is haram to the next world. They then have a choice, which is either to do what they want, seeking pleasure and avoiding pain, or else to discover the full science of what is halal and what is haram by following the way of Muhammad, may the blessings and peace of Allah be on him. If they make the first choice, they are at the mercy of their own desires and the illusory goals which the kaffir system, that is the Dajjal system, promises them. If they make the second choice, then they will arrive at the knowledge of what is halal and what is haram and they will know why something is halal or haram. If they follow the way of Muhammad, avoiding what is haram and doing what is halal, then they will arrive at an inwardly peaceful and outwardly balanced state of being, in which the very idea of kaffir insurance will be patently ridiculous. The one who does not follow the way of Muhammad and who subscribes to the kaffir producer consumer process, on the other hand, will inevitably think that insurance is a good idea, and waste as much money as he or she can afford on it.

People are encouraged to insure against every possible misfortune by the kaffir insurance companies simply because the more people insure, the greater the profit will be for the company. A kaffir insurance company cannot be described as a benevolent institution. It exists to make money out of other people's fears and anxieties. Of course it appears to be worthwhile when the event insured against actually takes place and you collect the money, but as we have already noted there are more human ways of dealing with loss and misfortune, which in the real muslim community take the form of voluntary giving out, without your having had to pay a premium as a condition precedent, either by individuals in the community who have been given more than they need by Allah, or else from the Bait ul Maal, that is the community's central fund into which all the minimal taxes required by Qur'an are paid, for the purposes of redistribution amongst those in need.

A brief historical study of muslim communities in the past clearly shows that when the people held to what is in Qur'an, and only paid the taxes which Allah had told them to pay, and immediately redistributed those taxes once they had been collected in accordance with what is in Qur'an, then those communities prospered. As soon as the people began to abandon what is in Qur'an, they were given leaders over them who likewise ignored Qur'an. The prophet Muhammad said that every people have the leaders that they deserve. As soon as these leaders began to gather extra taxes, and keep the proceeds either for themselves or out of anxiety, instead of redistributing them in accordance with what is in Qur'an, then the communities became divided against each other, ceased to prosper, and were eventually destroyed, as Allah has promised in Qur'an that every people who reject prophetic guidance will be destroyed.

When the companion of the prophet who was called Umar became khalif, he requested that he be told immediately the moment he strayed outside what is in Qur'an, so fearful was he of Allah and the Last Day. He was only too aware that the life transaction of Islam is its own insurance. A person once came to him and asked him to do the rain prayer, since there was a bad drought at the time. Umar, may Allah be pleased with him, replied that the reason for the drought was the fact that too many of the people in the community had become lax in following what is in Qur'an. In effect the outward drought was a reflection of the inward drought of lack of trust in Allah. When that trust was renewed, then the rain which is the mercy of Allah, came. The prophet Muhammad said that if any one were to have been a prophet after him, then it would have been Umar, may Allah be pleased with him.

The fact that many of the so called muslim but actually kaffir governments, which are, at the time of writing this, in control of the muslim lands because they are being supported by the kaffir colonisers who helped to put them there in the first place, collect taxes in addition to what is prescribed by Allah in Qur'an, and then refuse to redistribute them, is not only one of the reasons for the lack of prosperity in those countries, but is also a clear sign of the extent of the influence of the world wide kaffir system, that is the Dajjal system. Indeed it is a well known fact that the oil revenue of the muslim countries is used by the people who control it not for the benefit of the muslims, but to support the kaffir producer consumer system of the west and the east. This revenue, or at least a large proportion of it, is either invested in the large kaffir corporations or else deposited in the kaffir financial institutions where it collects interest. Since these kaffir corporations and these kaffir financial institutions are controlled by the free masonic elite of the kaffir system that is the Dajjal system, it follows that they are using the wealth of the muslims to destroy the muslims, for the principal aim of the free masons is to destroy the muslims, and to achieve world wide control through their business and finance systems, that is by establishing the kaffir system, that is the Dajjal system, world wide.

The prophet Muhammad said that every people has its trial, and that the trial of the muslims would be wealth. He also said that the downfall of the arabs would be black gold. This much is clear from what has happened to the rulers of Saudi Arabia, who in the name of Islam are busy establishing a kaffir police state, based largely on the kaffir models of the west. The prophet Muhammad made it quite clear that the leader of a muslim community should not be chosen to be the leader because his father was leader before him. Royal families are haram. A brief historical study of muslim communities in the past shows that as soon as these communities opted for dynastic rule, they became corrupted and were destroyed. It is quite clear that the leader of a muslim community should be recognised as such on the basis that his fear and knowledge of Allah are great, and that of all the people in the community he has the best understanding of what is in Qur'an, simply because he most embodies what is in it.

The corruption in the muslim lands is part of the inevitable process of life. To simply blame the Dajjal system for that corruption is not to see the whole picture. Clearly if the muslim leaders in the past had not already been prone to corruption, then the kaffir colonisers would have been unable to plant the seeds of the kaffir system, that is the Dajjal system, in the muslim countries in the first place, nor would those seeds have been able to sprout and grow.

The truth of the matter is that everything in life is subject to birth and death and growth and decay. Even the first community of Madina al Munawarra was subject to this cycle. The prophet Muhammad, may the blessings and peace of Allah be on him, foretold that the dynamic living Islam which that community enjoyed would only last in Madina for thirty or seventy years after he had died. He foretold civil war amongst the muslims, that is that muslim would fight muslim. He foretold that what had begun as a prophecy and a mercy, would become a khalifate and a mercy, would become a tyranny.

It is very easy to make Islam an instrument of tyranny, simply by systematising it, moralising it, and then inflicting that system and that morality, neither of which have anything to do with the life transaction brought by the prophet Muhammad, on other people who have no desire to be regulated by such a system and such a morality.

The prophet Muhammad also foretold that not all of his community would go astray. He said that towards the end of the world the muslims would be divided into seventy three different groups, and only one of those groups would have the living life transaction of Islam which he had originally brought. There can be no doubt that this one group, which has access to the living life transaction of Islam in all its rich simplicity, is formed of the awliya of Allah, that is the friends of Allah, the people whom Allah loves and who love Allah. The awliya of Allah are the ones who have preserved the living life transaction of Islam by the grace and guidance of Allah, in every time and age. They are recognised by the fact that people are drawn to them because of their wisdom and serenity, in the same way that people were drawn to the prophet Muhammad, and so real muslim communities form round them, as the first muslim community formed round the prophet Muhammad.

The real muslim community is simply the outward manifestation of what is inwardly in the heart of the wali, in the same way that the tyranny of the kaffir state is the outward manifestation of the inward darkness of the tyrants who control it. The heart of the wali is inwardly light and peace, and this manifests outwardly in the form of the harmonious and human transactions which characterise a real muslim community.

The awliya of Allah are not located in one place. As the ruh, that is the spirit form, pervades the entire body, so they are spread throughout the world. The awliya are the ruh of the world. Just as the body rots once the ruh has left it, so the world will come to an end once there are no longer awliya living in it.

The real muslim communities which form round the awliya of Allah are subject to the same cycle of birth and decay as the first muslim community of Madina al Munawarra. They begin with one man, the wali. The community then forms around him. The kaffirs try to destroy the community, but fail because Allah gives victory to those who trust in Him. Then the wali dies. There follows a period of balance during which the community continues to hold to what is in Qur'an, and is led by rightly guided men, who were the close companioins of the wali, and who received their knowledge of Allah by Allah through him. Then these companions die, and the community is led by those who were the companions of the wali's companions. Then they die, and gradually almost without anybody realising it, the community begins to lose the dynamism and living vibrancy which its first members possessed. With the continued passage of time the stage is reached where there is no longer a unified muslim community. They may still follow much of what is in Qur'an simply because that is what they have been born into, but many do this because it is what their fathers did, and not because they recognise Islam for what it really is. They no longer have what the original community which formed round the wali had. Everything in creation has its high point, and then thereafter there is a falling away. Basically a real muslim community which lives with the same zest for life, and with the same awareness of the true nature of existence, as the first community of Madina al Munawarra, only lasts for three generations. Then it is all over.

As quickly as one muslim community dies another is born somewhere else. The knowledge which the awliya possess, and which does not come from books, is transmitted person to person. Once a wali has transmitted that knowledge to another wali, then that wali takes that knowledge wherever he or she goes. In this way this knowledge has always been kept alive from the time of the prophet Muhammad up until now. Not every wali has a muslim community forming around him or her. Allah often hides who the awliya are as a protection for them. In those times during the alternating cycle of iman and kufr when kufr is in the ascendancy, the awliya remain hidden. Their job is simply to keep that knowledge alive, and to ensure that the chain of transmission remains unbroken. When the time arrives when iman is in the ascendancy, as it is now, then the awliya emerge into the open, and real muslim communities form around them, and there is nothing the kaffirs can do to stop them, because Allah gives victory to the ones who trust in Allah, and the awliya and those who follow the awliya are the ones who really trust in Allah. They cannot do other than trust in Allah because of the knowledge of Allah which Allah has given them. Allah said on the lips of the prophet Muhammad, may the blessings and peace of Allah be on him, that whoever makes war on a wali of Allah, Allah makes war on them.

Naturally there are ignorant people who claim to be walis when they are not. They deal in esoteric information and pseudo wisdom, but not in real knowledge of Allah. They are usually recognisable because they are concerned with personal reputation, that is they are more concerned about what other people think about them than what Allah knows about them, and because they usually charge money for the information which they pass on, and because outwardly they do not follow the existential life pattern of the prophet Muhammad, even in very essential matters such as doing the prayer, and because inwardly they do not have the light and wisdom which only a wali of Allah is given by Allah, and because, in the final analysis, they do not have idhn to teach, that is they do not have the permission of Allah to teach. One great wali in the past said that the one who speaks with idhn, his words are heard by creation, but the one who speaks without idhn, he is no more than a dog barking. Idhn is from Allah and His Messenger.

The true awliya are recognisable by a number of signs. Outwardly they embody the way of Muhammad in every respect. Inwardly they have a light which bathes and cleanses the hearts of those who sit with them. They have the best of manners and are human and compassionate. They have great wisdom and knowledge, which they share without charging a fee. They fear only Allah. They love Allah. They have gnosis of Allah, which is not the same as possessing information about Allah. Their selves have been purified. Allah loves them, and when Allah loves them, as Allah said on the lips of the prophet Muhammad, then He is the tongue with which they speak, and the hand with which they grasp, and the foot with which they walk. When you see them, it is as if you see instruments moved by divine decree.

The awliya are the complete antithesis of the free masons. The free masons are the elite of the kaffirs. The awliya are the elite of the muslims. The free masons only want power. The awliya only want

Allah. The free masons exploit and tyrannise the people they control. The awliya illuminate and liberate the people they serve. Both the free masons and the awliya are necessary to the creational process, which works by the dynamic interplay of opposites. You have to see which of the two opposites you belong to. If you are a kaffir go and join the free masons, because they receive the best of their world and the worst of the next world. If you are a muslim go and join the awliya, because they receive the best of this world and the best of the next world. The choice is yours right now.

The life transaction of Islam is the best insurance in the world. It guarantees provision in this world, and the Garden in the next world, for the one who embodies it with sincerity. The minimum that you have to do to ensure clothing, food and shelter, is five prayers a day. The minimum that you have to do to ensure the Garden, is to affirm that there is no god only Allah and that Muhammad is the messenger of Allah, in the moment; and to do five prayers in the day; and to fast during the month of Ramadan in the year, and to pay the zakat tax once every year; and finally, if it is possible, to do the hajj, that is the pilgrimage to Makkah, at least once in your life time.

These five essential actions, the five pillars of Islam as they are called, are not only all you need to do to reach the Garden, but are also the basis of a balanced life on this earth which inevitably leads to knowledge of Allah. They alone can transform the heart of the one who does them, and make it peaceful. Of course the more that you embody of the way of Muhammad, the more you gain from it, since there is great wisdom in everything which the prophet did, and this wisdom is only available for the people who do likewise. Ultimately, Allah is in the expectation of His slave. You will receive from Allah what you expect from Allah. Every one gets what they want. It is related that there was a man who on the Last Day was told that he was for the Fire. He replied, "Which is greater, my wrong actions or Allah's forgiveness?" Because he had this expectation of Allah, he went to the Garden.

The truth of the matter is that Allah could not show His mercy and forgiveness if no one had wrong actions. To the one who seeks knowledge of Allah, right action and wrong action are the same, because he or she learns from both. If the one who trusts in Allah is wise then he or she does not get stung in the same place or in the same way twice. For the one who desires to see the face of Allah, and that vision is possible in this world and in the Garden within the Garden in the next world, Allah is his or her only concern. The object in life for such a person is not to avoid the Fire and reach the Garden, but solely to see the face of Allah. The only way to reach the stage when and where Allah will give you this vision, if He wishes it, is by following the way of Muhammad.

The danger for the one who neither desires Allah, nor longs for the Garden, nor dreads the Fire, is that he or she will worship Islam instead of worshipping Allah, that is he or she will mistake the means for the end. The one who makes this mistake kills the living life transaction of Islam stone dead, and makes a religion out of it, that is a constricting web of do's and don't's which has nothing to do with the way of Muhammad. This is what the Jews and the Christians have done to the teachings of their respective prophets, Moses and Jesus, on whom be peace, and unfortunately some of the muslims have also made a religion out of the teaching of the prophet Muhammad, may the blessings and peace of Allah be on him, in fulfilment of his prophecy that some of the muslims would follow the example of their predecessors, meaning the Jews and the Christians, faster than a lizard makes for its hole.

If you wish to follow the way of Muhammad, learn from those who have travelled it, and not from those who have made a religion out of Islam. The ones who best know the way of Muhammad are the awliya, because they best embody it. The one who desires knowledge should only take it from the one whose actions are the same as his or her words. So in reality you have two choices. Firstly you may choose between iman and kufr. If you choose iman, then secondly you may choose between the living life transaction of Islam, which thrives round the awliya and which inevitably leads to knowledge of Allah and the Garden, or the dead religion of Islam which is kept alive by the people of book knowledge and mental morality and which leads nowhere. The choice is yours right now.

It is clear that a mumin's insurance, that is the living life transaction of Islam and trust in Allah, is accompanied by a vibrant awareness of the Unseen and of what comes after death. Kaffir insurance is the opposite of this. To the kaffir, death is not merely a doorway which leads from one world to another world. To the kaffir, death is the ultimate misfortune which is accordingly to be insured against. This is because the kaffir does not know what death is, or what lies on the other side of death. Even if he or she is told, the teller will not be believed. Life insurance also appears to be necessary to the kaffir because of his or her anxiety about provision and shelter in old age. In many ways this anxiety is well grounded in a fragmented kaffir society, because the young abandon the old, and leave them to fend for themselves, often alone. This is the complete antithesis of the real muslim community where life insurance policies are completely unnecessary, because everyone looks after each other, from birth to death.

Another inevitable result of the fragmentation of kaffir society, and especially a kaffir society which makes people want stuff because they have been conditioned to want it in order to keep the consumer producer process in business, is that there is a lot of what the kaffirs call crime. It is practically inevitable that the people who do not fear Allah and the Last Day, and who cannot get what they have been conditioned to want from the kaffir consumer producer process by legal means, will turn to crime. As we have already seen this criminal activity is not discouraged, or rather its true causes are not eliminated, because it gives a lot of people who work for the kaffir legal system a reason for living and a steady income. It also provides an added incentive to make people insure. As we have already seen, the insurers do not lose out, because they have fixed the insurance system so that they receive more in premiums than what they pay out in claims, and then these profits are further swelled by investing them and earning interest. Thus we see that the kaffir insurance system appears to be necessary, because it performs a costly service in a fragmented society where people do not trust each other. The average kaffir is obliged to trust in the average kaffir insurance company, which is not trustworthy, because in the final analysis its directors have the annual profits in mind, and not the welfare of their customers.

Anyone who has read the terms of insurance policies and studied the law which governs the interpretation of those terms, will know that the policies are designed to cover as little possible misfortune as they can in practice, whilst appearing and purporting to do the opposite in theory.

The kaffir insurance system is another of the important sub systems in the kaffir system, that is the Dajjal system. Whereas the kaffir legal and medical systems make their money out of the actual misfortunes of people, and misfortunes which have often been created by the way in which the Dajjal system is operated at that, the kaffir insurance system goes one step further and makes its money out of the fear people have for misfortunes which only might happen.

The illusory need to insure, which derives from groundless anxiety, and the need to insure, which arises out of the inevitable detrimental results of a kaffir society which is fragmenting, are both the children of ignorance as to how existence works, and of lack of trust either in Allah or in other people, and in truth these two trusts are the same trust. This state of affairs is in direct contrast to the reality of the mumin whose only insurance is trust in Allah, a trust which is manifested by his or her following the guidance which Allah has sent, and which is contained in Qur'an and the way of Muhammad. The prophet Muhammad, may the blessings and peace of Allah be on him, said that if you really trusted in Allah, you would live like the birds who go out in the morning with nothing, and return to their nests in the evening with nothing, and who in the meantime have been fed. He also said that whoever does five prayers a day is guaranteed food, clothing and shelter by Allah. The prophet himself could not go to sleep at night if there was money in his simple house. Accordingly he was what the kaffirs call bankrupt at the end of each of his days as a prophet.

The reality of provision is that Allah is the Provider, and He remembers those who remember Him as is promised in Qur'an. The reality of provision is that in the fifth month of pregnancy the ruh, that is the spirit form, is breathed into the foetus, and at that time it is written what his or her provision will be in the world, whether he or she will be happy or sad, when he or she will die, and whether he or she is for the Fire or the Garden. The whole matter is decided even before you were born. Once you are born whatever is coming to you comes at its appointed time, and whatever is not coming to you does not come. That is why Allah says in Qur'an that what is written for you cannot be avoided, and what is not written for you cannot be reached. That is why Allah says in Qur'an do not exult in what you are given, and do not grieve for what you are not given.

One of the companions of the prophet Muhammad asked him, "Are we on a matter which is completed, or are we on a matter which is not completed?" The prophet replied, may the blessings and peace of Allah be on him, "We are on a matter which is already completed. The pen has stopped writing, and the ink is dry." The kaffir tries to make a nonsense of this by conjuring up visions of an idiot sitting and doing nothing and waiting for his or her provision to fall out of the sky, or of another idiot who blindly walks across the road without looking to see if there is a car coming. This shallow kaffir concept, which is labelled predestination, has nothing to do with the true nature of existence. Your going out and getting things, and your taking precautions to avoid mishaps, your every breath, are all part of what has been written for you. You cannot do other than what is in your heart, your every move is already decided, but whenever you are faced with a choice you have to make the decision. Right now the choice is yours, but once it has been made, and looking back on it, perhaps you will see that you could not have made any other decision. Allah is the doer of you and your actions, and you are answerable for your actions on the Last Day, and depending on what actions you choose in this life, you will be for the Fire or for the Garden in the life after this.

It is sheer ignorance of this state of affairs which induces the kaffir not only to rely on his or her own actions rather than on Allah, from whom all actions come, but also to insure against what is defined by kaffir insurance terminology as risk. In reality there is no such thing as risk, just as there is no such thing as luck. Allah's mercy is greater than His wrath, and the way of Islam is the means to taste His mercy and avoid His wrath.

The reality of the kaffir insurance business system, and indeed of all the kaffir manipulation control finance systems, is that they are carefully designed to involve as many people as possible more fully in the kaffir producer consumer process, and to make as much money as possible out of that involvement. The kaffir insurance system plays a vital role in the functioning of the commodity markets which deal in raw materials from the mineral, vegetable and animal kingdoms, in bulk and in the future. These markets buy and sell crops which have not yet grown, metals which have not yet been mined, and livestock which has yet to be born. By dealing in the future like this, the profit margin is increased, whilst possible losses occasioned by unforeseen events are insured against, the premiums for the insurance being paid out of the large profits which have been made by paying the producers of the commodity in question a lower price in advance than the price which the buyer would have had to pay if the goods actually existed at the time of buying. This is yet another example of how the kaffir system creates a quite unnecessary pattern of activity in order to make money from it. The winners are those who operate the markets and the insurers. The losers are the people at the bottom of the company pyramid, who in fact do all the hard work.

Behind this pattern of activity of buying and selling in the future, a pattern of activity which is not permissible for the muslims, is not only sheer greed, but also a deep existential anxiety about provision. The muslim who does not have this anxiety, buys and sells what exists in accordance with the way of Muhammad, which clearly states that dealing in the future like this is haram, that is unfruitful, and that a trader should not make more than thirty per cent profit on all essential goods. It is because the muslim only deals in the present, and not in the future, and because he or she trusts in Allah, and the other muslims that he or she deals with, that insurance in the muslim business world is totally unnecessary.

If kaffir insurance was not a valid financial proposition, the kaffir insurance companies would not exist. The amounts which they are prepared to pay out, and the circumstances in which they are prepared to make payment, are all carefully calculated, so that overall payments out are a great deal less than the total amount of premiums received and invested. Because of the large profits which they make, they can afford to use the kaffir civil legal process to their advantage, either by employing kaffir legal experts to achieve the court decision which conveniently limits their liabilities in claims over which there is a dispute, or by offering sums which are less than what they should be really paying out, because they know that the person or company insured cannot afford to take them to court, and will therefore have to accept their offer. When the situation is such that both parties in a dispute over an insurance claim can afford to go to court, then of course this means continuity of work for the people involved in the kaffir civil legal process. This is yet another example of how the interlink between the sub systems of the kaffir system that is the Dajjal system ensures that they keep each other busy, by providing work for each other.

Once a person or company has taken out an insurance policy, or for that matter entered into a hire purchase or mortgage agreement or borrowed money from the bank, then this means that that person or company is committed to keep working in the kaffir producer consumer process, in order to keep up the payment of the premiums, or the hire purchase, mortgage or overdraft repayments. The more you insure, and the greater the financial commitments which you incur, the harder you have to work to pay them off, and accordingly the more you are trapped and enslaved by the kaffir producer consumer process. The kaffir media systems are used with devastating effect not only to encourage people to consume generally, but also, more specifically, to live beyond their present means. Once they have fallen into this trap it is then relatively simple to create money out of nothing, by charging them interest on the money which they owe. In effect you are provided with some of the goodies which the kaffir system that is the Dajjal system promises you, now, but at the price of having to pay much more for them than you would have had to pay if you could have bought them outright in the first place. The main purpose of these have it now pay later techniques is to create debts, because then the interest on the debts can also be collected. Furthermore this kind of transaction encourages the buyer to insure the goods, especially if we are talking about something expensive rather than something cheap, because there is nothing more frustrating than having to continue to pay for something which has been written off, especially if you are being charged interest. The chances are that the thing, whatever it is, will not be written off. This will mean that you have not only had to pay interest on the original debt, but also will have incurred the additional expense of the insurance policy. By inflating the cost of goods in the kaffir society by these methods, the free masonic controlling elite ensure that the people they control continue to be enslaved by the consumer producer system, whilst making a profit out of them.

The activity of the kaffir finance institutions makes the accumulation of vast pools of wealth a reality. Even a million one pound premium payments by a million small time policy holders, gives the company a million pounds. In the present complex kaffir states of the western world of course the actual figures are not mere millions, but run into hundreds and thousands of millions. What has been said of the kaffir insurance companies applies equally to the kaffir hire purchase finance companies, and to the kaffir building societies, and especially to the kaffir banks.

Of all the kaffir finance institutions, the kaffir banks accumulate the most wealth, because they not only charge interest on debts, but also encourage people to save money, if they have it to save, and to deposit whatever they save in the banks. Although the banks pay interest on money in deposit accounts, they can not only invest that money so as to receive more from it than what they have to pay out on it, but also they have most of the money which is lying in the current accounts to play with, and on this money they have to pay no interest at all. Thus whatever return they receive by investing current account money is all profit. The banks have found in practice that on average out of every thirteen pounds lying in the bank, there is only ever an actual demand by the clients of the bank for one of those pounds in cash. This leaves the bank with twelve pounds out of every thirteen to play with. The overall sum which the banks have to play with is phenomenal, because all the other kaffir finance institutions, and all the business corporations and concerns, and most of the people in the street, deposit their money with the banks. The banks are the means by which vast pools of wealth are accumulated.

The banks are controlled by free masons. The giant corporations of the kaffir producer consumer system, that is the Dajjal system, are controlled by the free masons. The governments of the kaffir states are controlled by the free masons. It follows that the free masons can use the vast pools of wealth which have been accumulated by the banks to finance those projects which will provide business for their large corporations, and furthermore this activity will be sanctioned by official government approval and permitted by the kaffir legal system. These large projects, which affect the lives of all those who work in them, are decided upon without asking all those who have been affected whether or not that is what they want. The project is set in motion, and the people who work in it work because they need the money, not because they necessarily believe in the project. Naturally the free masonic controlling elite decide on those projects which are profitable to them. In effect any project is profitable to them, firstly because the people who do the work are paid less than the money which is received by the company which employs them, and secondly because the money which they do earn has to pass through the banks, who then use whatever is not being spent by the client to finance yet another project.

The kaffir system, that is the Dajjal system, is a self perpetuating system. Once it has people working in and for it, their activity generates more activity, and all this activity generates money. The large corporations and companies do not really exist. They merely provide an effective facade to disguise the activities of the free masons who control them, and an illusory structure within which the people who work for them are trapped. Using the large kaffir corporations and companies as a front, the free masons channel the vast amounts of money to which they have access to finance the social projects which ensure continued profits for themselves, and which ensure the continued subservience of the people who are caught up in working in those social projects.

It is clear from this perspective that the kaffir taxation system is in fact just one more kaffir finance system, which ensures that people do not have too much money to play with, and are accordingly obliged to keep on working in the kaffir producer consumer process. Once the taxes have been collected, and their overall bulk and effect is disguised by giving them different names, and by taxing not only income but also any transaction where capital is gained or transferred and where consumer items are purchased, the money which has been accumulated in this way can then be used to finance the social projects of the free masonic ruling elite's choice. Thus for example the free masonic controlled government will give the juicy contract to the free masonic controlled building corporation to build all the buildings needed to house all the activities of the bureaucratic infra structure which is used by the government to control the country which it rules.

The argument, which states that since the government has been elected by the people, therefore it follows that the government policies are the policies which the people want and support, is nonsense. Firstly, the government which is publicly elected is not the real government. It is just a figurehead government, which distracts the attention of the people away from the real ruling elite who are the free masons. Secondly the reality of the kaffir election process today is that the figurehead government is always elected by a minority of the actual people in the kaffir state in question, even though it has been elected by a majority of those who bothered to vote. The reason why so many people do not bother to vote is because they at least have an inkling of the fact that they have no real choice in the matter. They are presented with a limited choice of apparently acceptable candidates, usually not more than two, both of whom make promises which they usually never keep, and neither of whom necessarily represent the views of those who end up voting for them, simply because there is no one else to vote for. The people are encouraged to vote, through the kaffir media system, on the basis that since it is their country, they should have a say in who rules it, but in fact they can only choose someone who has his name on the ballot slip, and the only people who ever get their name on the ballot slip and get elected are the people who secretly or unwittingly support the activities of the free masonic ruling elite.

Whoever the people vote for, or even if they do not vote, which means that they do not wish to be governed by any of the candidates standing for election, the so called government still gets elected, and the real ruling force behind the facade of the election pantomime, that is the free masonic ruling elite, remains in power. Of course some kaffir states do not even bother with elections. Instead the figurehead ruler claims to have the interests of the people at heart, and calls the country a people's republic to prove it, although this meaningless statement changes nothing.

The people who really rule the kaffir states of today are the people who control the kaffir finance and business institutions, that is the free masons. The free masons decide what the social projects are to be. The free masonic controlled business institutions carry out those social projects, enslaving the working population within those social projects in the process. The free masonic controlled finance institutions finance these projects.

The key kaffir finance institution is the free masonic controlled kaffir banking system since it handles the life blood of the consumer producer process, that is money. The importance of the banking system lies in the fact that it enables transactions between different countries using different currencies to take place. As a result of these international transactions, money itself becomes a commodity. As well as making money by charging commission every time one currency is changed into another currency, money can also be made simply by buying and selling different currencies at strategic intervals. These transactions are very magical since often no money actually changes hands, and yet by buying and selling on the same day, a profit can be made and recorded on the computer bank balance. This activity is very similar to what happens on the stock exchange, which is ostensibly the place where companies and corporations raise finance to finance their operations, by promising to pay the share holder a dividend, that is interest, on the money which he or she is effectively lending to the company. This method of raising money is attractive to the corporation or company, because it may work out cheaper than borrowing it from the bank. This method of lending money is attractive to the shareholder, because if the company or corporation makes large profits, then the annual return on the loan will probably be greater than the interest which would have accrued if the money loaned had been deposited with the bank.

What in fact happens is that the different shares, like the different currencies, become commodities in themselves. You can buy and sell them. You can buy and sell them for different reasons. You can buy and sell them to gain or relinquish control of the company or corporation whose shares they are. This works by virtue of the reasoning that if you are providing most of the finance for the company or corporation then you should have the final say in how it is run. Naturally the free masons have a controlling interest in all the important corporations, because only they have access to the funds which are necessary to acquire such an interest. This system of control by owning the bulk of the shares of any large business concern means that the free masons can take over virtually whoever they want, simply because they can provide whatever price is needed to achieve this object. Once they have a controlling share, they can then staff that company or corporation with their own people. This is one way in which the Dajjal takeover manifests.

The usual reason for buying and selling shares is simply to make money by investing it wisely, or to raise money quickly if you need it. Another reason for buying and selling shares is to make a quick profit without actually having had to part with money at any stage in the transaction. Like the gambling which goes on in the currency exchange, it all happens on paper, or on the computer screen. The favourite techniques are to buy shares, even though you do not have the money to pay for them, hoping to sell them again at a higher price, before the time for your original payment falls due. Alternatively you can sell shares which you do not possess, in the hope that you can buy them from someone else at a lower price than what you will be paid for them, and before the time arrives when you are meant to be handing them over to the person to whom you originally sold them before you had them. In both these cases you make a profit from nothing except skilful juggling. Of course if, like the free masons, you have the capital in the first place, then you can buy and sell shares at leisure, hoping that the market forces will eventually enable you to sell for more than you bought, or to buy for less than what you will sell.

It is in the commodity, stock and money exchanges that the power struggles for control of the kaffir producer consumer system, that is the Dajjal system, are conducted. It is from these power struggles that money is made. Thus even at the very tip of the producer consumer pyramid, the principle of divide and rule is applied. The main division is between those who control and those who are controlled. In financial terms this is the difference between those who lend money, and those who borrow money. Any large corporation in its infancy has to borrow money in order to grow. One of the ways in which this is done is to borrow money from one source, then to go to another source and borrow more money using the sum you have already borrowed as security for the second loan. Having in effect doubled your money on the strength of nothing, you then go to another source and borrow more money again using the money you have accumulated thus far as security. This process can usually be repeated up to eight times in succession by a corporation which is sufficiently large enough to command a good credit rating. Having amassed sufficient funds by this method, the corporation then has to embark on a business venture which will reap sufficient profits to pay back all the loans and the interest thereon. In order to do this its controllers must be ruthless, and all the successful ones are.

There comes a time when a successful corporation has generated enough activity, and accrued sufficient capital not to have to borrow any more. At this stage it can begin to take over other smaller corporations and companies, either by agreement or by sharp dealing on the stock exchange. There comes a point where the really large corporations have amassed enough capital in enough different countries to be able to have their own banking system, which works independently from, but not in competition with, the main kaffir banking system. In effect the multi national corporation bank is in a position to pursue all the profitable activities of kaffir banking, such as loaning money on interest and financing profitable projects for a price, whilst being released from the liabilities which they would incur if they still relied on the main kaffir banking system, such as having to pay bank charges every time large sums of money were transferred from one country to another, and being subject to exchange control regulations.

By having their own banks, the multi national corporations ensure their freedom to act. Since they and the main kaffir banking system are not in competition with each other, because all the chief controllers concerned are free masons, the money which the large multinational corporations expend, finds its way into the main banking system, which can then make it grow by lending twelve thirteenths of it at interest, or by investing that proportion profitably on the stock exchange.

The main kaffir banking system does not stop creating money out of nothing at this stage. Firstly, the money which has been created by charging interest can then be loaned out again and thus accrue further interest. This process continues ad infinitum. Secondly, the man who borrows a thousand pounds for example, will probably put some of it in the bank. Although to him it is a minus amount, in the sense that it is not really his to spend because he will eventually have to pay it back, to the bank it is a plus amount in the sense that twelve thirteenths of what has been deposited can be loaned out again, or otherwise invested. This process can also continue ad infinitum.

Where small man in the street transactions are concerned the aforementioned banking practices are not significant, although when all the small transactions in the world are added together, it is clear that the kaffir banks make a considerable profit even out of these. Where these practices do become significant is in the large multi national transactions. Loans of several million dollars or pounds accrue much interest in a short time. This means that the subservience of the debtor to the loaning bank is correspondingly greater. It also means that the pool of wealth, which the loaning bank accumulates by multiplying it through charging interest on what is loaned, increases at such a rate that in the end it does not really matter whether or not a particular loan is repaid. No one in the bank is going to starve if the loan is not repaid. What is important however is that the bank is in a position to dictate to the borrower the conditions on which the obligation to repay loan or interest or both will be waived, and it is in an even stronger position to lay down further conditions under which further sums will be loaned, such as in what projects the new loans must be invested.

In effect by creating debt, the bank gains control over whoever has borrowed the money. The final expression of this fact is to be seen in the activities of the International Monetary Fund and of the World Bank. Basically the I.M.F. lends money to the so called developed countries of the west, whilst the World Bank lends money to the countries of the third world, that is the so called under developed countries. These two kaffir financial institutions have so much money, on paper at any rate, that it has no meaning as money. What it means is control over a great many governments of the world, for once you have a government in debt you can then tell it how to spend the money which you subsequently lend it. In this way the free masonic controlling elite of the kaffir system, that is the Dajjal system, attempt to control the world. The free masonic controlled banking system loans money to countries, and continues to loan to them even after they have become heavily indebted, and can never hope to repay all the money back, on the condition that it is spent on free masonically chosen projects, which are to be carried out by free masonic controlled business concerns. This is the reality of what is called neo colonialism. Although it is said that the countries in question have been given their so called independence, in fact this has only been granted once the country in question has become totally involved in the kaffir consumer producer process, and totally reliant on the kaffir banking system to finance that process.

The people who really rule the kaffir states of today are the people who control the major kaffir finance and business institutions, that is the free masons. Effective control is exercised especially by using the kaffir banking system to create debts by charging interest, which grow so large that they can never be repaid. In order to speed up the process of creating debts, the free masons, as we have already seen, create conflict situations out of which profits are made by selling goods needed by the sides who have been drawn into conflict, at a high price, and out of which debts are created by providing those goods on credit at interest. The conflict situations created by the free masons vary from manipulating market forces, especially in the commodity markets and on the stock and money exchanges, to engineering war on a large scale. This was the activity which both Ezra Pound and Hitler were aware of, and tried to prevent without any success.

The reason why Pound and Hitler failed to expose and destroy the activities of the free masons was because they were not aware of the true nature of existence. The true nature of existence is that nothing exists, only Allah. It follows that anything other than Allah only appears to exist if you give it reality. The way of Muhammad means that reality is given to Allah. The way of kufr means that reality is given to other than Allah. If enough people, who are at present enslaved in the kaffir system, that is the Dajjal system, and who are accordingly imprisoned by the kaffir view of existence, decide to follow the way of Muhammad, and accordingly to cease to give reality to what they have been conditioned to give reality by the kaffir educational and media systems, then the kaffir producer consumer process will collapse and cease to exist. The way to fight the kaffir system, that is the Dajjal system, is not to fight it, but to leave it. The way to leave the kaffir system, that is the Dajjal system, is to follow the way of Muhammad. The kaffir system that is the Dajjal system is already in an advanced state of collapse. Accordingly it is becoming easier and easier to abandon it, and follow the way of Muhammad. The choice is yours right now.

One of the main reasons why the kaffir system, that is the Dajjal system, is in an advanced stage of self destruction and collapse is that the money, which is the life blood of the consumer producer process, and which is the medium of control through debt by the kaffir banking system, is only worth the paper it is printed on. As the life blood of the producer consumer system it is totally anaemic. It only succeeds in its role as a medium of control through debt by the kaffir banking system because enough people think it is worth something. It only has the value which people ascribe to it, but it has no inherent value. The endless discussions on the illusory topic of inflation, and the futile attempts to resolve the illusory problem of inflation are only decoys, smoke screens and red herrings, to disguise the fact that it is not a question of money losing value, simply because it has no real value in the first place. The reason why money has absolutely no value today, other than the illusory value which the great majority of people are conditioned to give it, is on account of the way that it is handled by the kaffir banks. In order to appreciate this fact, it is necessary to look at what money was, before the present kaffir banking system was first introduced.

Money used to be made principally of gold or silver. Since it was made from these precious metals it had inherent value. The first banks were formed to look after other people's money by keeping it in a safe place, although of course even at this stage money still had a palpable and valuable form. The practice arose whereby when someone deposited gold or silver in the bank, the banker would give the depositor a written receipt, whereby he promised to repay the gold or silver when that receipt was presented to him. The practice then arose that these receipts became transferable. Thus the depositor of the gold was able to buy goods to the value of the gold in the bank, by giving his receipt to the seller of the goods. The seller of the goods could then take that receipt to the bank, and collect the gold, even though it was not he who had originally deposited the gold there. Since gold and silver are relatively heavy, and since paper is relatively light, the bankers then hit upon the idea of printing paper money. Any one who deposited gold and silver with them was given this paper money. That paper money could then be used in any number of consecutive transactions, the understanding being that anyone at any time who had these notes come into his or her possession could, if he or she wanted, take them to the bank and exchange them for the gold or silver which they represented. At this simple stage every paper note was backed by its equivalent amount of gold or silver. You could exchange one for the other at any time. It was at this stage that the bankers discovered that for every thirteen pounds of gold or silver only one was required by the customer to spend at any one time, which left the bankers free to loan or invest the other twelve pounds on interest, or otherwise, profitably. This meant that for every thirteen paper pound notes, only one needed to be backed by gold, and this is what happened. It was no longer the case that every paper note referred back to its equivalent in gold or silver. Instead, for every pound's worth of gold or silver which the banks had, thirteen paper pound notes were printed. At this stage however you could still go into the bank, produce a paper pound, ask for a pound's worth of gold, and get it. Provided that not everyone tried to exchange their paper money for gold or silver at the same time, the banks were safe, even though in fact not all the paper money was backed by gold any more. At this stage, in real terms, money was only worth one thirteenth of what it used to be worth.

Gradually people became so used to using paper money, that no one even thought of going to the bank and asking for gold or silver in exchange. Everyone believed that the paper money was worth what it said it was worth on its two sides, that is its face value. At the same time the volume of the banks' business was increasing, as the origins of what is today's consumer producer process began to get under way and become established. This meant that it was creating more and more money, not by printing more bank notes, but by charging interest. Debt owed to the banks grew on paper in the ledgers, as the interest ticked up, but the money created in this way had no connection with the money which was already in existence, and which was backed by gold in the proportion of one gold to thirteen paper. In effect money was being created out of nothing, and this out of nothing money was not even being manifested in the form of pound notes, but merely being given reality by being recorded in a ledger, or as today, in the computer. This put the banks in a more precarious position. If everyone decided to draw their paper money out of the bank at once, the banks simply would not be able to produce it, simply because the volume of money, which was recorded as existing in the ledgers or in the computer, was so much greater than the number of printed money notes in actual circulation. Thus at this stage there were two credibility tricks which the banks had to play on the growing number of customers, who were needed by the banks for both profit and manipulation purposes. The first trick was to fool everyone into thinking that all the paper money was still backed by gold, even though people no longer tried to change paper notes for their gold equivalent. The second trick was to fool everyone into thinking that all the money, which existed according to the computer and ledger records, actually existed in the form of paper notes. Neither of these illusions created by the free masonic magician bankers was real, but as long as the great majority of the population thought they were real, then the whole magical but totally illusory system continued to work, and indeed continues to work today.

Clearly the greatest danger to the free masonic banking system was and is that too many people would ask for too much paper money at the same time. In order to regulate this supply and demand difficulty, people like Keynes came up with new theories of economics designed to replace the victorian theories of laissez faire, which could only, and had only, worked in a situation where real money with inherent value was being used. Basically Keynes drew people's attention to the fact that the demand for paper money in the hand could be regulated, by making spending and saving either more or less attractive, by raising or lowering the bank rate, that is the rate at which interest would be charged on loans and paid out on savings deposits. Very simply the higher the rate, the more it costs to borrow and the more interest you will receive on your savings deposits. Accordingly high interest rates encourage people to spend less and save more. Conversely low interest rates encourage people to borrow and therefore spend more, and to save less because if money is not going to grow very quickly, you might as well spend it. In effect Keynes's theories of economics appeared to achieve two things. When applied to the kaffir producer consumer process, they could be used to regulate the pace and extent of business activity, by making it more or less profitable. Secondly they were used to regulate the demand for paper money, by regulating the pace and extent of spending and saving.

Today there has been a further development in the bankers' attempts to ensure that not too many people ask for money which does not exist in paper form, but only in the computer memory, at the same time. Basically they are attempting to make it unnecessary to have money at all. This is done by encouraging not only cheque transactions, but also the increasing use of plastic cards transactions. The way that the plastic card transaction works is that when you produce your plastic card, which contains information as to your identity, together with the bank's guarantee that it will honour your financial commitments incurred by using that card, then a record of that information is made and sent to the bank together with the relevant details of the transaction, and the bank debits your account and credits the account of the person from whom, for example, you have bought the goods. In this kind of transaction no money passes hands. All that happens is that figures are juggled about in the computer memory bank. As more and more of these transactions occur and become commonplace, paper money ceases to have relevance. If this way of transacting is carried out to its ultimate and logical extent, then there will be no demand for paper money at all, because all transactions will be carried out via the plastic card, and the monetary result recorded in the bank's computer. Plus here, minus there. The aim of the free masons is to have the plastic card system operating throughout the world, because that will mean that everyone is dependant on their banking service, and that will mean that everyone is that more easy to control.

We see therefore that the influence of the kaffir system, that is the Dajjal system, through its kaffir banking system, has almost reached the stage where paper money is not only worthless, but also it does not matter that it is worthless, because everyone depends on the banks for their services in conducting their financial transactions. Furthermore, we have seen how the people in a kaffir society are encouraged to spend more than they have, and accordingly to become indebted to the kaffir finance institutions, especially the banks. This ensures continued dependance on the free masonic controlled kaffir banking system, whether by the man in the street, at his local branch, or by the government of a country developing the kaffir system in that country, at the World Bank or I.M.F. It is at this stage that the actual extent of the indebtedness is seen to be irrelevant. After all it only exists in the computer. What is important is the dependance on that banking system, for the greater the dependance on it, the greater the manipulation control it exercises, and accordingly the greater is the influence of the kaffir system, that is the Dajjal system, over the world.

The degree of that control and that influence can be measured by the fact that if you merely closed down all the banks for a little while, the whole kaffir consumer producer process would collapse.

The aim of the free masons is to perfect the kaffir system, that is the Dajjal system, by involving everyone in the producer consumer process, as far as their work and consumption of goods is concerned, whilst ensuring the smooth running and overall balance of activity in that process, by having everyone and every business concern dependant on their kaffir banking system. In effect they wish to arrive at the stage where the people of the world are completely caught up in one synchronised and unified field of activity, that is economic activity. If this aim were to be achieved, there would of course be only one currency, which would not even take the form of paper money, but which would be identified solely in terms of computer credits and debits. Ideally everyone would have their basic needs taken care of, but of course some would have them taken care of better than others, and the free masonic ruling elite would have them taken care of best of all, as has always been the case. This would mean that everyone would be comfortable in the free masonic idea of paradise now on earth made fact, but they would be completely unprepared for what comes after death.

Fortunately we know from Qur'an and the Hadith that this illusory dream will never be realised. There must inevitably be a collapse in the kaffir system, that is the Dajjal system, before the free masons' ideal can ever be made to happen. The social decay, which accompanies the way in which the kaffir system, that is the Dajjal system operates, means that the people who are most exploited by the system will cease to play the consumer producer game long before this dreamed of unified economic organism can become fact. The point in time is bound to be reached when enough people realise that the money in their pockets and the money recorded in the computer memory is absolutely worthless. This will mean that they will cease to become dependant on the kaffir banking system, and this will happen long before everyone has been issued with their plastic card. Most important of all is the fact that the present resurgence of Islam means that more and more people are severing connections with the kaffir system, that is the Dajjal system, and are ceasing to be trapped by that system. The more people cease to give reality to that system, the more it ceases to exist. As the number of real muslims grows, and as they begin to reunite, so the controllers of the Dajjal system will try to wipe them out. These attempts will find their most extreme expression when Dajjal the individual has appeared, and leads his army against the muslims who have gathered round the Mahdi.

This final and ultimate conflict between the two opposites, kufr and iman, which is referred to in other writings as Armageddon, will result in the death of Dajjal the individual and his followers, and indeed of the whole Dajjal system, thanks to the reappearance and intervention of the prophet Jesus, on whom be peace. The period of unified and peaceful muslim rule, in accordance with what is in Qur'an, under the Mahdi, the rightly guided leader of the muslims, will then commence.

The mumin understanding of economics is utterly opposite to that of the kaffir system of economics. This is because it is based on an understanding of the true nature of existence. The mumin knows that only Allah exists, although this knowing differs from person to person. Some know it intellectually and others know it through direct witnessing. It follows that the mumin knows that since money does not really exist, it is worth nothing, right from the start. To the mumin money is just a medium of exchange, but not a commodity. There is thus absolutely no point in hanging on to it whatsoever, and since the mumin has no anxiety about provision and shelter, his economics, as

112

we have already seen, are based on giving out in the knowledge that whatever he or she gives out will be returned by Allah ten times over.

There is no need for the muslims to amass capital in the way that the kaffir banks do, because their capital is the generosity of Allah, which is limitless. There is no need for the muslims to borrow and lend on interest, because Allah's interest is far higher than anything they could hope to charge, that is one thousand per cent. There is no need to manipulate people by getting them into debt, because since the body politic of the muslim community is unified there is no body of people within it who seek to control and manipulate and exploit the others. The only elite in the muslim community are the awliya, whose stations are greater than the others because they fear and love Allah more than the others, and because of their great knowledge of Allah and therefore of how existence works, they know that the more they serve the others, and the more they give out in the name of Allah, the more Allah will look after them and give them what they want.

Muslim economics is based on trust and on giving out. It is dynamic and free flowing. There is no need for Keynesian control techniques. Kaffir economics is based on exploitation of others and retention. It is static and stagnant. It stinks.

Given the dynamic nature of muslim economics, it comes as no surprise to learn that the value of money, in the time of the first muslim community of Madina al Munawarra, was based not on how much gold or silver it could buy, but on how much grain it could buy. Since grain was readily available, unless there was a severe drought, and could be grown by anyone, it followed that it could not be used to make the value of money fluctuate, in the way that the limited markets of gold and silver are manipulated to raise and lower the apparent value of today's worthless money, almost at will. This meant that the basic value of money remained stable in Madina al Munawarra, and accordingly there was no such thing as what the kaffirs call inflation. Furthermore, since the taxes required by Qur'an were so low, it followed that there was no stimulus to make people raise their prices in order to beat the effects of the taxes, as happens in today's modern so called advanced kaffir state. Accordingly prices remained stable, and so again there was no inflation caused by rising prices. Furthermore, since it is not permissible to make more than thirty per cent profit on essential goods, muslims in that first community did not raise prices too high out of sheer greed, if they feared Allah and the Last Day. Since the value of money was stable, and since prices were stable, it followed that wages were stable, so there was no inflation caused by excessive wage demands, as happens today in the so called modern kaffir state. Finally, since Allah expressly forbids the charging of interest, saying more than once in Qur'an that it is haram, and will take you to the Fire if you indulge in it, it follows that there was no opening for the kind of business institution which today lives off other people's indebtedness to it, by charging interest.

Allah says in Qur'an that the first community of Madina al Munawarra was the best community that has ever lived on the face of the earth. It follows that in order to know how to live, it is necessary to see how they lived. Having seen this, it is possible to apply their way of doing things to the way we do things today. The kaffir argument that their way of life is now out of date, and does not and can not apply to the twentieth century, is palpably weak. The scenery and the props may change, but the human situation remains the same, and the way of the first community is the best way of dealing with it. Following the way of the first community of Madina al Munawarra does not mean religiously imitating their way of life in every detail. It does not mean having to abandon today's technology, where that technology can be usefully used, and used with the discrimination between what is halal and what is haram.

The way of the first community was based on what is in Qur'an and on the example of the prophet Muhammad who was described by his wife Ayesha as being Qur'an walking. Records of that example still exist today, both in Qur'an and the Hadith collections, and in human beings, notably the awliya, who have had the existential way of living of the prophet and the knowledge which goes with it transmitted to them, person to person, from the time of the prophet Muhammad and the first community up until the present day, without a break in that chain of transmission.

The nature of Qur'an is such that the guidance in it can be applied to any situation. Where there is no specific mention of what to do in the situation you find yourself in, it is still possible to see what to do by doing ijtihad. Ijtihad is the process whereby you see what to do in the light of what you know of what is in Qur'an and Hadith and of the way of Muhammad. To begin with it is a conscious thinking process, but as the heart becomes more finely tuned and illuminated, ijtihad becomes a reflex action. You know what to do and what not to do in the moment, and without having to think about it. If you are not sure about something all you have to do is open Qur'an, and you will see the ayat that is the sign which contains the answer. Thus it is not only muslim economics which is dynamic, but the whole way of life in whatever sphere.

The nature of phenomenal existence is such that there is a constant and dynamic interplay of many opposites, which is always in motion and never exactly repeats itself, even though patterns and cycles are clearly recognizable. You are part of that interplay. You are not separate from it. The way of Muhammad is the way of knowing what to do in that interplay, so that you never fight it, but go with it. By living in this way you arrive at knowledge of Allah from whom this interplay of opposites originates and returns, not only in the very beginning, and at the very end, but also in every moment. By living in this way you arrive at knowledge of yourself, and you find that the whole of existence is your self, and whoever knows their self truly they know their Lord, Allah. When you live in this way and with this knowledge then you are a human being, who acts with humanity. You are pleased with Allah and Allah is pleased with you, and in this state you enter the Garden.

The result of the way in which all the kaffir sub systems and institutions in the kaffir system, that is the Dajjal system, work and operate, is to depersonalise and dehumanise the human transaction. Where in the past people used to give to each other, now they charge each other for services rendered. Where once common sense, generosity, wisdom, flexibility, and above all humanity, used to characterise human transactions, now the rules of the various systems which together form the Dajjal system are applied with automatic and unfeeling inflexibility. The complementary descriptions, which are given to affirm and promote this system, do not in the least accord with what is actually going on. The words, the conditioning, the programming, the explanations, the reasons are no more than a web of illusion which has been spun by the controlling elite of the Dajjal system, the free masons, so that they can entangle and enslave the many, and feed off them as they struggle to free themselves. The kaffir system, that is the Dajjal system, uses people until they are of no further use to that system. They are treated like robots, because machines are much easier to control than human beings. Machines submit to whatever you do with them without complaint, provided they are kept in running order. You do not have to behave like a human towards a machine, because machines can not respond like humans. You just use them until they have come to the end of their working life, and then you get rid of them and carry on with replacements.

115

It is only possible to treat people like robots, because half the people in the kaffir system, that is the Dajjal system, already are robots. The so called people who are completely happy with the kaffir system, that is the Dajjal system, are the people who have been taken over, are the living proof of the manifestation of Dajjal as a world wide social and cultural phenomenon, and Dajjal as an unseen force, will be the people who recognise, support and follow Dajjal the individual when he appears, will be for the Fire. The people who abhor the kaffir system that is the Dajjal system are the human beings who have not been taken over, who if they are not already muslims will be muslims, Insha Allah, who will recognise, support and follow the Mahdi when he appears, who are for the Garden.

You belong to either one group or the other group, and there is no third group. You cannot extricate yourself from the creational process of which you are a part, and which is based on the dynamic interplay of opposites. There is no escape. Hiding your head in the sand will not change who you are, but will merely make it extremely difficult to see where you are ultimately going.

There is one other definable group who in fact belong with the kaffirs. This group is the munafiqoon, that is the people who say they are muslim but who in reality are kaffir, because they do not trust in Allah, and they do not follow the way of Muhammad, even though they know that it exists. The munafiqoon are a part of the Dajjal system, and when the army of the Mahdi confronts the army of Dajjal the individual, they will be with the followers of Dajjal. In the next world they will be in the deepest part of the Fire, because they did not act on what they knew in this world, that is they did not follow the way of Muhammad, even though it was there for them to follow, and they knew it.

The people who are attempting to follow the example of the prophets who came before the prophet Muhammad, such as the ones who brought the Vedas, Buddha, Moses and Jesus, are in a difficult position. The sincere among them wish to worship Allah, but it is impossible for them to worship Allah in the way that Allah has indicated that He is to be worshipped, because the books they have are not the original books which their prophets were given, and because the existential life pattern of those prophets has been lost for ever. It follows that the people who still attempt to follow the way of these prophets in this day, will never have true knowledge of Allah, because this knowledge only comes to the one who embodies what has been revealed to the prophet whom he or she follows. If the existential life pattern of embodying that teaching has been lost, and if the teaching itself has been lost by having been changed by corrupt people in the past, then it is not possible to follow the original life pattern of the prophet concerned or his original teaching, and therefore knowledge of the Real, Allah, is not possible, by holding to the remnants of those earlier teachings.

Allah says in Qur'an that everything in creation worships Allah, only some people do not realise this. Every atom in existence is sustained by the power of Allah and is proof of Allah and worships Allah. All the kingdoms in the phenomenal world and in the Unseen praise Allah, but only man is capable of having gnosis of Allah. The one who has this knowledge of Allah worships and praises Allah with a greater understanding than any other created being or thing. The atoms in the body of a kaffir bear witness to the limitless perfection and splendour of Allah, but with his or her words and actions the kaffir denies the very existence of Allah. The atoms in the body of one who trusts in Allah bear witness to the limitless perfection and splendour of Allah, and so do his or her words and actions, and what is more the one who trusts in Allah knows this, and has knowledge of Allah. The one who tries to follow the way of one of the prophets who came before the prophet Muhammad, is somewhere in between these two opposites. The atoms in his or her body bear witness to the limitless perfection and splendour of Allah, but because he or she is not following a guidance which is still intact, it follows that only some but not all of his or her actions affirms this Reality and his or her understanding of what he or she is doing, and accordingly his or her understanding and knowledge of Allah, is therefore incomplete and inevitably partially distorted.

Only by knowing Allah can you truly worship Allah. The worship of Allah by the one who has gnosis of Allah is deeper than the worship of Allah by the one who only has an intellectual understanding of Allah, is deeper than the worship of Allah by the one who only has limited information about Allah, is deeper than the worship of Allah by the one who has distorted information about Allah, is deeper than the worship of Allah by the one who only worships Allah by virtue of the existence which Allah has given to him or her, but who consciously thinks that Allah does not exist.

The greater the knowledge that a person has of Allah, the more he or she realises that he or she knows nothing. Again and again in Qur'an Allah says that Allah knows and you do not know. One of the signs of ignorance is thinking you know when in fact you do not know. This is especially true of the kaffirs, but it also applies to those who are content to try and follow the distorted remnants of an earlier prophetic teaching, which is now defunct and not really for this time.

Those who have not yet had access to the living life transaction of Islam cannot be blamed for not following it. Allah says of the people who follow prophets other than Muhammad in this time, that those who worship Allah with sincerity have nothing to fear from Allah on the Last Day. Allah also says in Qur'an that once a person knows about Islam, no other way of life is acceptable to Allah. Surely the life transaction with Allah is the life transaction of Islam. The life transaction with Allah always has been the life transaction of islam. All the prophets embodied the life transaction of islam, one of whose meanings is acceptance of the way things are, including submission of the self in worshipping Allah, but the only life transaction of islam which is still intact today, and which is for today until the end of the world, is the life transaction of Islam which was brought by the prophet Muhammad, may the blessings and peace of Allah be on him, and right now the choice is yours.

The only viable alternative to the kaffir system, that is the Dajjal system, is the way of Islam. All other apparent alternatives never succeed in being established. Either these movements are rapidly eliminated and annihilated by and in the Dajjal system, or else they are reshaped and absorbed into the Dajjal system, or else they are in reality already part and parcel of that system, and any apparent conflict between the two is merely on the surface. The reason why Islam is the only viable alternative to the kaffir system that is the Dajjal system is that the way of Islam is diametrically opposed to the way of Kufr. They are opposites, and one of the secrets of life is that everything lies in its opposite. In the dynamic interplay of opposites, which is the creational process, the interplay between kufr and iman is such, that once you have one, you will inevitably have the other. Anyone who is awake sees that this is true not only of themselves, but also of other individuals, other families, other communities, other towns and cities, other countries and indeed of the whole world. Since, at the time of writing, the kaffir system that is the Dajjal system is the dominant force in the world today, it is inevitable that the life transaction of Islam must replace it tomorrow. Everything lies in its opposite, and there is no changing the way of Allah.

The only way of appreciating what the way of Islam is, is to become muslim if you are not one already, and to follow that way. No one can bring you to Islam and no one can take you away from it. Allah says in Qur'an that there is no compulsion in the life transaction. It is Allah who makes the straight way plain from the crooked one, and the straight way is the way of Islam, and it is as narrow as the edge between the two sides of a sharp sword. This is why the wise who take this way rely on Allah for success. It is Allah who expands the heart to Islam. You can not make people become muslim, even the ones you love. It is Allah who gives the ability to discern the differences between kufr and iman, and between what is displeasing to Allah and what is pleasing to Allah, and between what is haram and what is halal, and between what words and actions lead to the Fire and what words and actions lead to the Garden. Above all it is Allah who gives knowledge of Allah, to whom He pleases as He pleases. You will not acquire knowledge of Allah by looking for it, but only those who look for it will acquire it. That is, do not rely on your actions, but rely on Allah.

In reality everything is from Allah. The whole cosmos comes from and returns to Allah, and it does not contain Allah, but Allah contains it, and no form or idea in the seen or unseen worlds can be associated with Allah. Allah is not like anything. If you have an idea of Allah, Allah is not like that idea. You are the idea of Allah. The whole of creation is Allah's idea. To understand this you have to put your head on the ground before Allah. Until you have stood, and bowed, and prostrated, and sat in the presence of Allah in the same way that the prophet Muhammd stood, and bowed, and prostrated, and sat in the presence of Allah, you cannot begin to appreciate what the way of Islam is, nor can you begin to have real knowledge, that is knowledge of the Real, Allah.

The reason why the Jews and the Christians cannot have real knowledge, that is knowledge of the Real, Allah, is that they do not do the same prayer as the prayer that their respective prophets, Moses and Jesus, once did. The way that Moses and Jesus prayed, and the words that they actually used, have been lost for ever. The prayer of the muslims and the words they use are the same as the prayer of the prophet Muhammad, and the words that he actually used. When you recite Qur'an you recite the words which the angel Gabriel recited to the prophet Muhammad, may the blessings and peace of Allah be on him, and which the prophet Muhammad recited to his followers, may Allah be pleased with all of them.

In reality everything is from Allah. The cosmos is the manifestation of the Names and Attributes of Allah, which display the Beauty and the Majesty of Allah. All that people think good, and all that they think bad, is from Allah, by the decree of Allah. To have knowledge of Allah it is necessary to abandon all value judgements, and all mental moral judgements. It is necessary to stop thinking, so that you can let the heart take over. Existence does not cease when you stop thinking, rather you see it in a different light. Relax the mind and learn to swim. Clean the heart with rememberance of Allah, in order that you may find what is in it. Allah. In Reality there is only Allah. Allah said on the lips of the prophet, "La ilaha il'Allah means Me and only Me." Wherever you look, there is the face of Allah. Everything is passing away except the face of Allah. There is no reality, only the Reality. There is only Allah. Allah.

Allah guides whoever He wishes and Allah leads astray whoever He wishes. Allah gives life and Allah takes away life. Allah increases and decreases provision. Allah said, on the lips of the prophet Muhammad, may the blessings and peace of Allah be on him, "I send people to the Garden and I do not care, and I send people to the Fire and I do not care." Allah is the doer of you and your actions, and you are responsible for your actions. On the Last Day you will not be asked what others were doing, you will be asked what you were doing, and you will not question Allah, but Allah will question you, and depending on what you did in this world, and the intention behind what you did, and your expectation of Allah, and the mercy and wrath of Allah, you will be for the Fire or for the Garden. Allah has power over everything. There is no strength to do right or wrong action, except from Allah. There is no strength and no power, except from Allah. You are helpless, but right now the choice is yours.

The only way of following the way of Islam is to keep company with those who do their best to follow the example of the first community of muslims who gathered round the prophet Muhammad at Madina al Munawarra, the illuminated place where the life transaction is. Such a company will only be found round a person whom Allah loves, and who loves and fears Allah, that is a wali of Allah, a friend and lover of Allah. The wali of Allah is the one who, after the prophet Muhammad, comes nearest to embodying and understanding what is in Qur'an. The wali of Allah is a drop compared to the ocean of the prophet Muhammad, may the blessings and peace of Allah be on him. The wali of Allah is the best of guides because Allah guides the ones He loves, and no one is loved more by Allah than the awliya. The awliya are the ones to whom the living life transaction of Islam, and the knowledge which goes with it, have been transmitted in an unbroken chain of transmission, from the prophet Muhammad, person to person, to the awliya of today. It is the awliya of today who are the ones who know and follow the way of Islam. The greatest of them meet and talk with the prophet Muhammad in true dream and in vision, receiving confirmation and guidance whenever it is needed. Help comes to them from the prophet Muhammad in every moment. The awliya of Allah have gnosis of Allah which gives them certainty as to the true nature of existence.

There are three stages of certainty. The mithal, that is the likeness, of these three stages is that you are told of the fire in the forest, and without seeing it you believe the one who told you; then you see the fire in the forest and feel its heat, so that there is no room to doubt its existence; then finally you are the fire in the forest, utterly transformed and annihilated by and in it. In this final stage of certainty is the station of the greatest of the awliya, and the meaning of this station is that Allah loves them, and when Allah loves them, He is the tongue with which they speak, and the hand with which they grasp, and the foot with which they walk. It is because of this that their pleasure is Allah's pleasure, and their guidance is Allah's guidance, and they are the best of guides, and they cannot be associated with Allah who is the Guide. It is from amongst the awliya that the Mahdi will appear. The Mahdi will be the most rightly guided of guides, and all the real muslims will recognise that.

A distinction must be made between the living life transaction of Islam, which has been transmitted to and preserved by the awliya, and the dead religion of Islam which has been created and perpetuated by the people who obtain their knowledge solely from books. The awliya use books, but they do not rely on them. Their knowledge comes from fear of Allah and by the grace of Allah. If your knowledge does not come from the fear of Allah then you have been deceived. One of the great awliya in the past said to a man who relied solely on books, "You get your knowledge from the dead, but we get our knowledge from the Living who never dies." Another of the great awliya in the past said, "If the prophet Muhammad left my sight for a moment, I would no longer consider myself a muslim."

At best the ones who rely solely on books for their knowledge of Islam only ever reach the first stage of certainty. They will go to the

Garden, Insha Allah, but they are not the best of guides. The danger of following them is that you will end up worshipping Islam and not Allah, mistaking in effect the means for the end.

The way of Islam is so that you can have knowledge of Allah, and worship Allah, and the best knowledge of Allah is gnosis of Allah, and the one who has gnosis of Allah worships Allah with a deeper understanding of Allah than the one who only possesses information concerning Allah.

At worst the ones who rely solely on books for their knowledge of Islam will side track you away from Islam, because they do not always act on what they know. Only take your knowledge from the one whose actions and words are the same. In an ignorant age a person's words are mistaken for their actions. Such people do not act from certainty but out of expediency. They fear other than Allah and they do not fear Allah. They are confused and they confuse whoever listens to or follows them.

The prophet Muhammad said that there would be some people who would have Qur'an on their tongues, but not in their hearts nor in their actions. He said they would be the worst people on the face of the earth. These are the munafiqoon, the hypocrites, destined for the deepest part of the Fire. One of their signs is that they have no fear in their hearts that there may be hypocrisy in their hearts. They are recognizable in that they consider themselves experts of Islam, in the same way that the kaffir expert considers him or her self an expert in a particular field. Although they use so called islamic vocabulary, the institutions which they either initiate or support are modelled on the institutions of the kaffir system, that is the Dajjal system. In effect they are part and parcel of that system. Today they are to be found particularly in the muslim lands, whose governments are kaffir, and which are being controlled by the kaffir system, that is the Dajjal system. These munafiqoon are used by the corrupt governments to gain the people's acquiescence in and acceptance of these governments, by telling them that these governments are islamic. In the same way that the people of the western kaffir states are persuaded to accept the kaffir system, that is the Dajjal system, because they believe what the so called kaffir experts tell them, so the people in the muslim lands are persuaded to accept the infiltration of the kaffir system, that is the Dajjal system, in their countries, because they believe the so called islamic experts who tell them that the ways of the kaffirs, which their governments have adopted, are islamic. Allah does not show many people who the munafiqoon are, but no doubt as to their identity is left whenever there is a direct confrontation between kufr and iman, since at that point they side with the people of kufr and oppose the muslims. This is a sign of their ignorance and lack of trust in Allah, since the reason why they side with the kaffirs is that they think the kaffirs are going to come out on top.

The cerebral brand of islam which they advocate is nothing to do with the living life transaction of Islam, as embodied by the prophet Muhammad and the first muslim community of Madina al Munawarra, simply because they say one thing and do another. The religion of Islam which they have manufactured is really no more or less than kufr in disguise, in the same way that the modern religions of Judaism and Christianity are no more or less than kufr in disguise.

One of the most distinguishing features of these three pseudo religions is that they are all orchestrated by a hierarchical ruling elite of priests some, but not all, of whom are in fact free masons into the bargain. They do not oppose the kaffir system that is the Dajjal system, but rather they support it, often providing so called religious ceremonies to provide an aura of respectability and credibility to some of the kaffir rites and public occasions. In effect they are a part of the kaffir stage show which is put on for the benefit of the general public, in order to disguise the true nature of the activities of the free masonic ruling elite. Naturally there are members of each of these three official priesthoods who are sincere in their actions and worship of Allah, but if these people took the trouble to examine the respective teachings of their prophets, they would find that none of these prophets, nor indeed any prophet, ever initiated a priesthood who said you need us to reach Allah.

The real transaction with Allah is between you and Allah direct, and without any intermediary. Your whole life is between you and Allah. Those who have access to the living life transaction of Islam know this.

The teaching of the prophet Muhammad, may the blessings and peace of Allah be on him, is the only prophetic teaching which is intact today, because the awliya to whom this teaching has been transmitted are all muslims. You will not find gnostics of Allah, which is what the great awliya are, amongst the Hindus, or the Buddhists, or the Jews, or the Christians, because gnosis of Allah is only possible for the one who has access to, and follows, the prophetic teaching which is still intact. All the prophetic teachings which were once followed in their entirety long before the coming of the prophet Muhammad have either been lost or altered, and either successfully depotentised by the kaffir system, that is the Dajjal system, or incorporated into it, and this is also partially true of the people who have turned the original teachings of Islam into a mental moral dead religion.

The few Jews who can still claim to be direct descendants of the tribe of Israel which was led by Moses, and the Jews who are not Jews, that is the descendants of the Khazars or those who have interbred with other races, do not follow the existential life pattern which was embodied by Moses. The Christians do not follow the existential life pattern which was embodied by Jesus. The books on which the Jews, and the Jews who are not Jews, and the Christians, rely are unreliable, having been altered and censored by corrupt rabbis and priests in the past, who made changes in order to compromise with kaffir rulers, and in order to make a bit of money on the side. Furthermore in both cases it is not even the original book which has been changed: In the case of the Jews there was a point of time in their history when all existing copies of the Torah were utterly destroyed. They tried to get it back on paper, by gathering together all the rabbis who had committed different parts of it to memory, to see if whether between them all they had memorised the whole Torah. They had not. Still they put an edition together which contained as much as they could remember. It was this edition which was subsequently further altered by corrupt rabbis, who wished to bend the law which the Jews had derived from the original living life transaction of islam brought by Moses. In the case of the Christians it would seem that the Ngeel, that is the gospel, which was revealed to Jesus was never actually committed to paper. Certainly there is no book called the Gospel according to Jesus and written in Aramaic, which was his tongue, in existence today. If there is, the Christians are keeping very quiet about it. Instead their so called New Testament contains four official gospels, according to people who never even met Jesus, which contradict each other many times over, together with the teachings of Paul which openly contradict the original living life transaction of islam brought by Jesus. It is this book which has been altered by corrupt priests in the past who wished to embellish the original teachings of Jesus almost beyond recognition, and to make their new religion more amenable to kaffir rulers. Perhaps the most flagrant alteration is the insertion of the one and only reference to the Paulinian doctrine of the imaginary Trinity which was discovered by, inter alia, Sir Isaac Newton to be a forgery. According to the gospel of Barnabas, the Ngeel was not committed to paper, but was revealed to Jesus in vision, taking the form of a well of knowledge in his heart, from which he could draw as he wished.

This is not to say that there is no truth left in the books on which the Jews, and the Jews who are not Jews, and the Christians rely. There is truth in them, and some of their contents most probably correspond with the original books which were revealed to their respective prophets. They do not however contain the whole truth, and furthermore as well as having been censored, deliberate lies have been inserted. It is for this reason that they are not reliable.

The original Torah as revealed to Moses no longer exists. The original Ngeel, or gospel, as revealed to Jesus no longer exists. The people to whom the existential life pattern of these prophets was transmitted, person to person, without a break in the chain of transmission, are all long dead. The chain of transmission from Moses and Jesus has been broken and lost for ever. Even if you are filled with the greatest sincerity, you cannot follow the existential pattern of worship and behaviour which was embodied by Moses and Jesus, and Buddha and the bringers of the original Vedas for that matter, and the communities which formed around them, because that behavioural pattern has been lost for ever, and other falsified patterns put in its place, in their names and in the name of God.

The Qur'an is the only prophetic guidance on the face of the earth today which has not been changed one letter either by alteration, addition or subtraction. It is recorded as it was revealed. Allah has promised that it will remain intact until the end of the world. There is no doubt in it. It is utterly reliable. Even the most ingenious of kaffir so called scholars and orientalists have been unable to discredit it. Allah says in Qur'an that if you do not believe that the Qur'an is from Allah, then try and write something like it. Allah says in Qur'an that if the whole of mankind and all the jinn banded together, they could not produce the like of the Qur'an between them. Furthermore the existential life pattern of the prophet Muhammad and the community which formed around him has been preserved and transmitted, person to person, in an unbroken chain of transmission, right up until today.

If you believe in Allah and wish to worship Allah in the manner which Allah has indicated that He should be worshipped through his prophets, then you must find out what is in Qur'an, and follow the way of Muhammad, that is the living life transaction of Islam. Right now the choice is yours.

Each of the one hundred and twenty four thousand prophets who have been sent by Allah were sent for specific people, and at a specific time in the history of mankind. Some were sent for only a few people, some were sent for a particular tribe, some were sent for a particular nation, and only one was for the whole world. Noah for example only had nineteen followers at the time of the great flood, even though he lived for nine hundred and fifty years. Both Moses and Jesus were sent only for the tribe of Israel, so only Allah knows what the Jews who are not Jews, and the Christians who are not descended from the tribe of Israel, are up to today. Only the prophet Muhammad was sent with a guidance, a good news and a warning, for all people from the time Qur'an was revealed to him up until the end of the world. The times for all the prophets who came before the prophet Muhammad are now long over. The people for whom all the prophets who came before the prophet Muhammad were sent are now long dead. The time for following the way of the prophet Muhammad is now. The people for whom the prophet Muhammad was sent have either died during the last fourteen hundred years, or they are alive today, or they will live at some stage between now and the end of the world. The only way to follow the prophetic life pattern today is to follow the way of the prophet Muhammad, may the blessings and peace of Allah be on him and all who follow him, because his way is the only prophetic life pattern which has survived intact up until today, and which will continue to survive up until the time immediately preceeding the end of the world when Allah takes the arwah, that is the spirit forms, of all the muslims then alive from this world, leaving only the people who will live like animals until the end of the world.

The prophet Muhammad, may the blessings and peace of Allah be on him, is the first and the last of the prophets. He was in existence when Adam was still between water and clay. He is the seal of the prophets, confirming by Qur'an all the messages of the prophets before him, and thereby abrogating and completing those messages. Qur'an contains all that the teachings of the earlier prophets contained, and more. It is the final edition of the A to Z of existence, and its author, publisher and distributor is Allah, the Originator of all that appears to exist, and the One to whom all that appears to exist returns. Since the prophet Muhammad was the embodiment of Qur'an, that is Qur'an walking, he was the only complete and perfect man that existence has ever known, and he can not be associated with Allah, because Allah is One, alone without partner.

Allah was a hidden treasure, and He wished to make Himself known, so He created the Universe. When there was only Allah, before time space began, Allah took a portion of His light and said, "Be Muhammad." From this light of Muhammad all the source forms of everything that was ever to manifest either in the Unseen, or in the phenomenal world which is apprehended by the senses, were created. The source form of the man and prophet Muhammad was the first source form to be created. Since that time all the source forms created from the light of Muhammad by Allah have manifested, and continue to manifest, and will continue to manifest until the end of the world, in the Unseen and in the phenomenal worlds. Everything is made from the light of Muhammad. The light of Muhammad is from the light of Allah. Only Allah exists. Everything in the time space continuum is an illusion, is not what it appears to be. Do not curse the time space continuum, for it is Allah. Everywhere you look, there is the face of Allah. Everything is passing away except the face of Allah. Allah is as He was before the creation of the Universe, and He continues to be. There is only Allah. Say: Allah, He is One. Allah He is Ever continuing. He was not born from anything, and nothing is born from Him. And there is nothing like Him. Allah.

The reality of the prophets, may the peace of Allah be on them all, is that the next prophet only came when the teaching of the prophet before him had been lost. All the teachings of all the prophets, except for the teaching of the prophet Muhammad, have been lost. The prophet Muhammad is the last of the prophets before the end of the world. If you wish to follow the way of the prophets you have no choice but to follow the way of Muhammad. Right now the choice is yours and it is a very simple one to make, but a difficult one to put into practice.

The prophet Muhammad said that a time would come when to hold to the living life transaction of Islam would be like handling hot coals. That time has come. The people who control the kaffir system, that is the Dajjal system, are making it difficult to hold to the living life transaction of Islam. This is a test from Allah. The more Allah loves someone, the more Allah tests them. No one was tested as much as the prophet Muhammad, may the blessings and peace of Allah be on him, because no one has been loved as much by Allah as the prophet Muhammad.

The reality of the prophets is that they were all from Allah, and they all brought the same message, because there is only one Allah to know and affirm, and because the nature of existence, which derives from Allah, has always been essentially the same. This means that there is no competition between the prophets because they all affirmed One and the same Reality, Allah. In the same way there is no

127

competition between the awliya, because there is only Allah, and they know it with direct seeing. The knowledge, the knower and the known are One. The muslims are the only ones who recognise this. This is why only the muslims accept all the prophets, and make no distinction between them, all one hundred and twenty four thousand of them.

There is no way to worship Allah, as Allah has indicated He should be worshipped, except by following the way of Muhammad, may the blessings and peace of Allah be on him. Only by following the way of Muhammad will you be able to affirm the true nature of existence, and understand it, and know your self, and truly whoever knows their self knows their Lord. The whole Universe cannot contain Allah, but the heart of the one who trusts in Allah contains Allah, and the way to your heart is the way of Muhammad, may the blessings and peace of Allah be on him.

Either you are for the kaffir system, that is the Dajjal system, or you are against it. If you are against it, then you are for the way of Islam. If you are not against the way of Islam, and you must find out what it really is, because it certainly is not what the kaffir educational and media systems depict it to be, then you are for the way of Islam. No one can take you to Islam, and no one can take you away from Islam. Allah is in the expectation of His slave, and we are all slaves of Allah, and we all know that, because when Allah had created the source forms from the light of Muhammad He said to all the arwah, that is the spirit forms, of all the people who would ever come into and go out of existence, "Am I not your Lord?" that is "Alastu birabbikum?" and they all answered yes. Deep in the heart, the one who is mumin remembers this, whilst the one who is kaffir pretends it did not happen. The only way to realise the full extent of your being a slave of Allah, and this means that you will not be a slave of anything or anyone or any idea which or who appears to be other than Allah, is to follow the way of Muhammad, who was the perfect slave of Allah. He was so pure that he cast no shadow when he walked in the sunlight. When he laughed, light bounced off the walls. His sweat smelled of musk. He was immersed in rememberance of Allah in every moment. He was always in complete abasement before Allah. He was a complete and perfect man, and therefore his way is the best of ways. Right now the choice is yours.

It is not known when Dajjal the individual is going to appear. It is not known when the Mahdi, the rightly guided leader of the muslims, who walks in the footsteps of the prophet Muhammad, may the blessings and peace of Allah be on him, and who worships Allah alone and without partner, because he knows there is only Alah, is going to appear. They may appear in your life time, they may not. What is known is that there are only two basic ways of living while you are on earth. Either you follow the way of kufr, or you follow the way of Islam. Dajjal the individual will merely be the final embodiment of all that denotes the way of kufr. The Mahdi will be the final human embodiment of all that it is possible to follow in the way of Islam, for only the prophet Muhammad was in a position to be all of Qu'ran walking, may the blessings and peace of Allah be on him.

It is not possible to defer making your choice between the two alternatives until a later date, since once you know that you have a choice, it must be made. Right now the choice is yours.

Qur'an is crystal clear as to what will happen when the opposites meet: Allah gives victory to the ones who trust in Allah, over the ones who reject Allah. Qur'an is crystal clear as to what will happen to you after your death. If you trusted in Allah and followed the way of His prophet Muhammad, then you will be for the Garden. If you rejected Allah and refused to follow the way of His prophet Muhammad, then you will be for the Fire. For ever. Right now the choice is yours.

Once you know about the way of Muhammad, the living life transaction of Islam, no other life transaction is acceptable to Allah. Surely the life transaction with Allah is Islam. Right now the choice is yours.

From 'Umar, may Allah be pleased with him:

"One day while we were sitting with the Messenger of Allah, may the blessings and peace of Allah be on him, there appeared before us a man whose clothes were exceedingly white and whose hair was exceedingly black; no signs of journeying were to be seen on him and none of us knew him. He walked up and sat down by the Prophet, may the blessings and peace of Allah be upon him. Resting his knees against his and placing the palms of his hands on his thighs, he said, 'Oh Muhammad, tell me about Islam."

The Messenger of Allah, may the blessings and peace of Allah be on him, said, "Islam is to witness that there is no god only Allah and that Muhammad is the Messenger of Allah; to do the prayer; to pay the zakat; to fast in Ramadan; and to go on pilgrimage to the House if you are able to do so."

He said, "You have spoken truly." And we were amazed at him asking him and saying that he had spoken truly. He said, "Then tell me about Iman."

He said, "It is to believe in Allah, His Angels, His Books, His Messengers, and the Last Day, and to believe in the Decree, the good of it and the evil of it."

He said, "You have spoken truly." He said, "Then tell me about Ihsan."

He said, "It is to worship Allah as though you see Him, and though you do not see Him, yet truly He sees you."

He said, "Then tell me about the Hour."

He said, "The one questioned about it knows no more than the questioner."

He said, "Then tell me about its signs."

He said, "That the slave girl will give birth to her mistress; and that you will see the barefooted, naked, destitute herdsmen competing in constructing tall buildings."

Then he went, and I stayed for a time. Then he said, "Oh, 'Umar, do you know who the questioner was?"

I said, "Allah and His Messenger know best."

He said, "It was Gabriel, who came to teach you your deen."

It was related by Muslim.

From Abu Abdullah Jabir the son of Abdullah al Ansari, may Allah be pleased with them both:

"A man asked the Messenger of Allah, may the blessings and peace of Allah be on him, "Do you think that if I do the obligatory prayers, fast in Ramadan, treat as permitted that which is permitted and treat as forbidden that which is forbidden, and do nothing more than that, I shall enter the Garden?"

He said, "Yes."

It was related by Muslim.

Yahya related to me from Malik that he heard that the Messenger of Allah, may Allah bless him and grant him peace, said, "I have left two matters with you. As long as you hold to them, you will not go the wrong way. They are the Book of Allah and the Sunna of His Prophet."

It was related by Malik bin Anas.

You are on a journey. Your passage through this world is only a brief part of that journey, like a person who enters a room through one door, crosses it, and goes out through another door; or like a rider who comes to a tree, rests under it for a moment or two, and then continues his or her journey. Allah says in Qur'an that people will be asked how long their lifetime was in this world, and they will reply that it was only a short time, maybe a day or half a day. The prophet Muhammad, may the blessings and peace of Allah be on him, said that you should be children of the next world, not of this world, because this world is leaving you and the next world is approaching you. He also said, "Love whom you will, they will surely die. Do what you will, you will be judged accordingly." Right now the choice is yours.

You are on a journey. Truly everything comes from Allah and returns to Allah, willingly or unwillingly, via the Garden or via the Fire, including you. Right now the choice is yours. Wake up. Time is passing.

You are on a journey. The journey is to Allah.

ALLAH

When everyone is standing before Allah
On the Last Day
Allah will
Say
"Who is the King now?"

There is no god only Allah
Muhammad is the messenger of Allah.

Say: This is my way.
I call on Allah with sure knowledge,
I and whoever follows me.
Glory be to Allah.
And I am not of the idolaters.

QUR'AN: Sura Yusuf
Ayat 108

GLOSSARY OF ARABIC TERMS

ADAB: Inner courtesy coming out as graciousness in right action.

ADHAN: The call to prayer.

AHLU DHIMMA: Non muslims living in muslim territory and under the protection of muslim rule by virtue of the fact that they have agreed to pay the JIZYA tax.

AKHIRA: What is on the other side of death; the world after this world in the realm of the Unseen.

ALASTU BIRABBIKUM?: "Am I not your Lord?" The question which ALLAH asked all the ARWAH when they were first given form. They all answered, "Yes", including you.

ALLAH: The Lord of all the Worlds and what is in them, including you. ALLAH has ninety nine Names all of which are from and within the One, ALLAH. ALLAH, the supreme and mighty Name, indicates the One, the Existent, the Creator, the Worshipped, the Lord of the Universe. ALLAH is the First without beginning and the Last without end. He is the Outwardly Manifest and the Inwardly Hidden. There is no existent except Him and there is only Him in existence.

AL HAMDULILLAHI WA SHUKRULILLAH: Praise to ALLAH and thanks to ALLAH.

'ALIM: A muslim who has sound knowledge of the QUR'AN and HADITH, and accordingly of the SHARI'A and the SUNNA, and who puts what he knows into action.

AMIR: One who commands and makes the final decision; the source of authority in any given situation. When and wherever there is a group of MUSLIMS it is the Sunna to choose an AMIR from amongst themselves.

AQL: Intellect, the faculty of reason. The noun derives from the verb which means to hobble a camel.

ARWAH: The plural of RUH. Spirits.

AWLIYA: The plural of WALI. The friends of Allah, and those who have the greatest knowledge of ALLAH, which is MA'RIFA.

AYAT: A phrase structure of QUR'AN, and also a sign, both in the linguistic and semiotic sense. There are AYATS in the self and on the horizon.

BARAKA: Blessing. A subtle energy which flows through everything, in some places more than others, most of all in the human being. Purity permits its flow, for it is purity itself, which is light. Density of perception blocks it. Since it is light, BARAKA is intimately connected with the RUH.

BAIT UL MAAL: House of wealth. The treasury of the muslims where income from ZAKAT and other sources is gathered for redistribution.

DAJJAL: The ultimate embodiment of KUFR, manifesting as an individual, as a social and cultural phenomenon, and as an unseen force. Sometimes denoted by the term antichrist.

DEEN: The life transaction, the way you live and behave towards ALLAH. It is submission and obedience to a particular system of rules and practices. Literally it means the debt or exchange situation between two parties, in this usage the Creator and the created, or as some say between the conditioned and the unconditioned, the limited and the limitless, or the many and the One. ALLAH says in the QUR'AN that surely the DEEN with Allah is ISLAM.

DHIKR: Remembrance and invocation of ALLAH. All worship of ALLAH is DHIKR. Its foundation is declaring the Unity of ALLAH, prostrating before ALLAH, fasting, giving to the needy, and doing the pilgrimage. Recitation of QUR'AN is its heart, and invocation of the Single Name, ALLAH, is its end.

DINAR: A gold coin weighing 4.4 grams.

DIRHAM: A silver coin weighing 3.08 grams.

DUNYA: The world as it is imagined, inwardly and outwardly. It has been compared to a bunch of grapes which appears to be in reach but which, when you stretch out for it, disappears.

FARD: What is Obligatory in the SHARI'A. This is divided into FARDUN 'ALA-L-AYAN, which is what is obligatory on every adult muslim; and FARDUN 'ALA-L-KIFAYA, which is what is obligatory on at least one of the adults in the muslim community.

FASIQOON: Those who split and divide, either their selves inwardly, or existence outwardly.

FIQH: The formal study of knowledge, especially the practice of ISLAM. It is the science of the application of SHARI'A.

FITRA: The first nature, the natural, primal condition of mankind in harmony with nature, with the self inwardly, and with existence outwardly.

FUQAHA: The scholars of FIQH, who by virtue of their knowledge can give an authoritative legal opinion or judgement which is firmly based on what is in QUR'AN and the HADITH and is in accordance with the SHARI'A and the SUNNA.

FURQAN: The faculty of being able to discriminate between what is valuable and what is worthless, between what is fruitful and what is unfruitful, between what is good and what is bad for your self and others. One of the names of QUR'AN is AL FURQAN. To embody the SUNNA and follow the SHARI'A is FURQAN.

JIBRIL: The angel GABRIEL who was the means by which the QUR'AN was revealed to the prophet Muhammad, may the blessings and peace of Allah be on him.

GHAYB: The Unseen.

GHUSL: Washing the entire body with water in accordance with the SUNNA of the prophet Muhammad, may the blessings and peace of ALLAH be on him. It is necessary to have a GHUSL on embracing ISLAM, after sexual intercourse or seminal emission, at the end of menstruation, and after child birth; and before being buried when your body is washed for you. It is necessary to be in GHUSL and in WUDU before you do the SALAT or hold a copy of the QUR'AN. GHUSL is a purification both inwardly and outwardly.

HADITH: The written record of what the prophet Muhammad said or did, may the blessings and peace of Allah be on him, preserved intact from source, through a reliable chain of human transmission, person to person.

HADITH QUDSI: The written record of those words of ALLAH on the tongue of the prophet Muhammad, may the blessings and peace of Allah be on him, which are not a part of the Revelation of QUR'AN, preserved intact from source, through a reliable chain of human transmission, person to person.

HAJJ: The greater pilgrimage to the KA'ABA, the House of ALLAH in MAKKA, and the performance of the rites of pilgrimage in the protected area which surrounds the KA'ABA. The HAJJ begins on the 8th of DHU'L HIJJA, the twelfth lunar month of the muslim calendar. The HAJJ is one of the pillars of ISLAM, and is a purification outwardly and inwardly.

HAJRAT AL ASWAD: The Black Stone, a stone, which some say fell from heaven, set into one corner of the KA'ABA in MAKKA by the prophet Ibrahim, peace be on him, which the pilgrims in imitation of the prophet Muhammad, may the blessings and peace of Allah be on him, kiss, so unifying all the MUSLIMS throughout the ages in one place.

HALAL: What is permitted by the SHARI'A.

HARAM: What is forbidden by the SHARI'A. Also

HARAM: A protected area. There are two protected areas, known as the HARAMAYN, in which certain behaviour is forbidden and other behaviour necessary. These are the areas around the KA'ABA in MAKKA and the area around the Prophet's Mosque in MADINA, in which is his tomb, may the blessings and peace of Allah be on him.

HIJRA: To emigrate in the way of ALLAH to a place where it is possible to follow the way of Muhammad, may the blessings and peace of Allah be on him, and establish the DEEN of ISLAM as a social reality. Islam takes its dating from the first HIJRA of the Prophet, from MAKKA to MADINA.

HUDOOD: The limits. The boundary limits which separate what is HALAL from what is HARAM, as defined by ALLAH.

'ID: A festival. There are two main festivals of the muslim year, on the first day of which 'ID prayers are prayed.

'ID AL ADHA: A four day festival at the time of HAJJ. The 'ID of the (greater) Sacrifice, it starts on the 10th day of DHU'L HIJJAH, the day that the pilgrims sacrifice their animals, remembering the sacrifice which the prophet Ibrahim, on him be peace, was prepared to make, and the sacrifice which he made instead.

'ID AL FITR: A three day festival after the month of fasting, RAMADAN.

IDHN: Permission or Authority, either to teach, or to fight JIHAD in the way of ALLAH. IDHN is from ALLAH and His Messenger, may the blessings and peace of ALLAH be on him.

IHSAN: The inward state of the MUMIN who is constantly aware of being in the Presence of ALLAH, and who acts accordingly. IHSAN is to worship ALLAH as though you see HIM, and though you do not see HIM, know that He sees you.

IJTIHAD: Exercising personal judgement. The faculty of deciding the best course of action in a situation, which is not expressly referred to in the QUR'AN and HADITH, and then choosing a course of action which is close to the SUNNA and in accord with the SHARI'A. Very useful when dealing with technology.

IMAM: The one who leads the communal prayers. In the first Muslim community of MADINA AL MUNAWARRA, the AMIR was the IMAM.

IMAN: Trust in ALLAH and acceptance of His Messenger, may the blessings and peace of Allah be on him. IMAN grows in the heart of the one who follows the way of ISLAM. IMAN is to believe in ALLAH; His Angels; His Books; His Messengers; the Last Day; and the Decree of what is good and what is evil. Thus IMAN is the inner knowledge and certainty in the heart which gives you TAQWA and TAWBA and the yearning to know more.

ISLAM: The prophetic guidance brought by the Prophet Muhammad, may the blessings and peace of Allah be on him, for this age for the people and jinn who desire Peace in this world, the Garden in the next world, and knowledge and worship of Allah in both worlds. The five pillars of ISLAM are the affirmation of the SHAHADA; doing the SALAT; fasting RAMADAN; paying the ZAKAT; and doing the HAJJ if you are able. The peak of ISLAM is JIHAD. A person enters ISLAM by saying the SHAHADA in front of at least two witnesses, and having a GHUSL either directly before or after this.

ISNAD: The written record of the names of the people who form the chain of human transmission, person to person, by means of which a HADITH is preserved.

ISRAFIL: The angel who will blow the Trumpet which heralds the Last Day.

IZRAIL: The angel who takes the RUH from the body at the moment of death.

JAHILIYYA: The time of arrogance and ignorance which precedes the time when the

136

way of ISLAM is established as a social reality. Anyone who does not have wisdom suffers from JAHILIYYA.

JALAL: ALLAH's Attribute of Majesty.

JAMAL: ALLAH's Attribute of Beauty.

JIHAD: The fight in the way of ALLAH against KUFR. Inwardly, the greater JIHAD is the fight against the KUFR in your own heart. Until your heart is purified, you are your own worst enemy. Outwardly, the lesser JIHAD is the fight against the KAFFIR who attempts to subvert or destroy the practice of ISLAM.

JINNAH: The Garden, the final destination and resting place of the MUSLIMS in the AKHIRA, once the Day of Reckoning is past. JINNAH is accurately described in great detail in the QUR'AN and the HADITH.

JINN: Beings made of smokeless fire who live in the Unseen. Some are MUMIN, some are KAFFIR, some are the followers of SHAYTAN, and we seek refuge in ALLAH from the accursed SHAYTAN.

JIZYA: The annual tax paid by all adult males of the AHLU DHIMMA, who are guaranteed the protection of the muslims in return.

KA'ABA: The House of ALLAH, in MAKKA, originally built by the prophet Ibrahim, peace be on him, and rebuilt with the help of the prophet Muhammad, may the blessings and peace of Allah be on him. The KA'ABA is the focal point which all muslims face when doing the SALAT. This does not mean that ALLAH lives inside the KA'ABA, nor does it mean that the muslims worship the KA'ABA. It is ALLAH whom the muslims worship, and ALLAH is not contained or confined in any form or place or time.

KAFFIR: The one who denies the Existence of ALLAH and who rejects His Prophets and Messengers, and who accordingly has no peace or trust in this life, and a place in the Fire in the next life. Shaykh 'Abd al Qadir al Murabit writes, "Kufr means to cover up reality: kafir is one who does so. The kafir is the opposite of the mu'min. The point is that everyone knows 'how it is' – only it suits some people to deny it and pretend it is otherwise, to behave as if we were going to be here for ever. This is called kufr. The condition of the kafir is therefore one of neurosis, because of his inner knowing. He 'bites his hand in rage' but will not give in to his inevitable oncoming death." (Quranic Tawhid. Diwan Press. 1981).

KHALIF: One who stands in for someone else, in this case, the leader of the muslim community. In the first muslim community of MADINA AL MUNAWARRA, the KHALIF was the AMIR was the IMAM.

KHARAJ: Taxes imposed on revenue from land or the work of slaves.

KHULAFA AR RASHIDUN: The rightly guided KHALIFS, Abu Bakr, 'Umar, 'Uthman and 'Ali, may Allah be pleased with all of them.

KUFR: To cover up reality, to deny ALLAH, to reject His Messengers.

KUTUB: Books. Often meaning the Books revealed by ALLAH to His Messengers.

LUBB: A core. This term is used in the QUR'AN to indicate people who have great understanding in the core of their being, the heart. Those who have LUBB are capable of worshipping ALLAH with deep knowledge and attaining MA'RIFA.

MADINA AL MUNAWARRA: The city to which the prophet Muhammad made HIJRA, may the blessings and peace of Allah be on him, and where the revelation of QUR'AN was completed. The first MUSLIM community was established in MADINA AL MUNAWARRA, and ALLAH says in QUR'AN that this is the best community ever raised up from amongst mankind. Their hearts and actions were illuminated and enlightened, may Allah be pleased with all of them, by ALLAH and His Messenger; and MADINA AL MUNAWARRA is still illuminated by the presence of the ARWAH of those of them who are buried there, especially the prophet Muhammad, may the blessings and peace of Allah be on him.

MAHDI: One who is rightly guided. The prophet Muhammad, may the blessings and peace of Allah be on him, said that there would be a mahdi every hundred years who would revive the DEEN of ISLAM, and that the last of them would be the MAHDI who would fight the DAJJAL until the prophet Jesus, peace be on him, returned to this world and killed the DAJJAL.

MAKKA: The city in which the KA'ABA stands, and where the revelation of QUR'AN commenced.

MAKRUH: Disapproved of without being forbidden.

MALA'IKA: The Angels, who are made of light and glorify ALLAH unceasingly. They are neither male nor female. They do not need food or drink. They are incapable of wrong action and disobeying ALLAH and do what ALLAH commands them to do. Everyone has two recording angels over them who write down their actions and none of this escapes the knowledge of ALLAH.

MAMNU'A: What is prohibited in acts of worship in the SHARI'A.

MA'RIFA: Gnosis, the highest knowledge of ALLAH possible to man or woman. It is to directly witness the Light of the Names and Attributes of ALLAH manifested in the heart. Shaykh 'Abd al Qadir al Murabit writes, "Gnosis, the central knowledge, for it is knowledge of the self, is a proof to the one who knows it and this is its glory and its supremacy over all others. By it its possessor knows the universe, how it is set up and its underlying laws in their action, their qualities and their essences. His knowledge of the Universe is his own self knowledge, while his knowledge of his own self is direct perception of his own original reality, the adamic identity. Everything he has comes from Allah. He never sees anything but he sees Allah in it, before it, after it. There is only Allah in his eyes as there is only Allah in his heart." (Qur'anic Tawhid. Diwan Press. 1981).

MA'SH'ALLAH: It is the will of ALLAH. It is what ALLAH wants.

MIKAIL: The angel in charge of the Garden.

MIZAN: Balance, in life, inwardly and outwardly. MIZAN is also used to indicate the means by which actions and intentions will be measured on the Last Day. Shaykh 'Abd al Qadir al Murabit writes, "Al-Mizan. Its meaning is the justice and harmony of all creation and therefore of time/space and therefore of us and events. It is the meaning of the Garden and the Fire, of the balance between the matrices, it is what was called in the ancient Tao-form of Islam in China, yin/yang. It is the secret of the contrary Names. It is what we are born and die on, and which turns our acts and intentions into realities to be weighed on the Day of the Balance." (Qur'anic Tawhid. Diwan Press. 1981).

MUDD: A measure of volume, one both hands cupped full, a double handed scoop.

MUFSIDA: What invalidates acts of worship in the SHARI'A.

MUFSIDOON: The mischief makers. Those who say they are putting everything right, when in fact they are only creating disorder.

MUHSIN: The MUSLIM who has IHSAN, and who accordingly only gives reality to the Real, ALLAH. Only the MUHSIN really knows what TAWHID is. A WALI of ALLAH once said, "The difference between the Kaffir and the Muslim is vast. The difference between the Muslim and the Mumin is greater still. The difference between the Mumin and the Muhsin is immeasurable," Not only in inward state, but also in outward action.

MUMIN: The MUSLIM who has IMAN, who trusts in ALLAH and accepts His Messenger, may the blessings and peace of Allah be on him, and for whom the next world is more real than this world. The MUMIN longs for the Garden so much, that this world seems like the Fire by comparison.

MUNAFIQOON: The Hypocrites. Those people who outwardly profess ISLAM on the tongue, but who inwardly reject ALLAH and His Messenger, may the blessings and peace of Allah be on him, and who side with the KAFFIR against the MUMIN. The deepest part of the Fire is reserved for the MUNAFIQOON.

MUNKAR and NAKIR: The two angels who question the RUH in the grave after the dead body has been buried, asking, "Who is your Lord?; "Who is your Prophet?; "What is your Book?; "What was your Deen?" The KAFFIR will be confused. The MUMIN will have the best reply.

MUSHRIQOON: The idol worshippers, those who commit SHIRK.

MUSLIM: One who follows the Way of ISLAM, not abandoning what is obligatory in the SHARI'A, keeping within the HUDOOD of ALLAH, and embodying as much of the SUNNA as he or she is able, through study of the QUR'AN and HADITH followed by action. A MUSLIM is, by definition, one who is safe and sound, at peace in this world, and guaranteed the Garden in the next world.

MUSTAHAB: What is recommended, but not obligatory, in acts of worship in the SHARI'A.

MUTAFIFEEN: The cheaters. Those who give short measure and demand more than a fair price.

NABI: A prophet. A man rightly guided by ALLAH and sent by ALLAH to guide others. Altogether there have been one hundred and twenty four thousand prophets in the history of mankind. The last prophet before the end of the world, the Seal of the Prophets, is the PROPHET MUHAMMAD, may the blessings and peace of ALLAH be on him.

NAFS: The illusory experiencing self. You as you think you are. When the NAFS is impure, it is an illusory solidification of events obscuring a light, the RUH. When it has been completely purified, the NAFS is RUH.

NAR: The Fire of Jahannam, the final destination and place of torment of the KAFFIROON and the MUNAFIQOON in the AKHIRA, once the Day of Reckoning is past. Some of those MUSLIMS who neglected what is FARD in the SHARI'A and who did grave wrong action without making TAWBA will spend some time in the Fire before being allowed to enter the Garden, depending on the Forgiveness of ALLAH who forgives every wrong action except SHIRK if He wishes. NAR is accurately described in great detail in the QUR'AN and HADITH.

NAWAFIL: What is voluntary in acts of worship in the SHARI'A.

N'SH'ALLAH: If ALLAH is willing. If ALLAH wants it.

NUR: Light. ALLAH says in the QUR'AN that ALLAH is the Light of the heavens and the earth.

NURI MUHAMMAD: The RUHANI Light of Muhammad, may the blessings and peace of ALLAH be on him.

QADR: The Decree of ALLAH, which determines every sub atomic particle in existence, and accordingly whatever appears to be in existence. One of Allah's Names is AL QADIR, the Powerful, the One who does whatever He wants. Again and again QUR'AN reminds us that ALLAH has power over everything and that ALLAH does what He wants.

QABR: The grave, experienced as a place of peace and light and space by the RUH of the MUMIN, who sees his or her place in the Garden in the morning and the evening; and experienced as a place of torment and darkness and no space by the RUH of the KAFFIR, who sees his or her place in the Fire in the morning and the evening. After death there is a period of waiting in the grave for the RUH until the Last Day arrives, when everyone will be brought back to life, assembled together, and sent to the Garden or to the Fire. So do not have your body cremated.

QIBLA: Direction. Everyone has a direction in life. The direction which the MUSLIMS face when they do the prayer is towards the KA'ABA in MAKKA. This direction is what distinguishes the MUSLIMS from everyone else, who have every direction except the QIBLA.

QUR'AN: The Recitation. The last revelation from ALLAH to mankind and the JINN before the end of the world, revealed to the prophet Muhammad, may the blessings and peace of ALLAH be on him, through the angel Gabriel. The QUR'AN amends, encompasses, expands, surpasses, and abrogates, all the earlier revelations revealed to the earlier prophets, peace be on all of them. QUR'AN was and is the greatest miracle given to the prophet Muhammad by ALLAH. QUR'AN is the uncreated word of ALLAH. Whoever recites QUR'AN receives knowledge, for it is the well of wisdom in this age.

QUTB: The pole or axis of the universe, only understood by the one who has attained it.

RAMADAN: One of the pillars of ISLAM. It is the ninth lunar month of the MUSLIM calendar during which all adult MUSLIMS who are in good health fast from dawn to sunset each day. During the first third of the fast you taste ALLAH's Mercy; during the second third of the fast you taste ALLAH's Forgiveness; and during the last third of the fast you taste freedom from the Fire. The QUR'AN was first revealed in the month of RAMADAN during the Night of Power, which is one of the nights in the last third of RAMADAN. The fast of RAMADAN is a purification outwardly and inwardly.

RASOOL: A Messenger, a prophet who has been given a revealed Book by ALLAH. Every Messenger was a Prophet, but not every Prophet was a Messenger.

RUH: The spirit, formed of pure light, the Light of ALLAH.

RUHANI: Pertaining to the RUH.

RUSOOL: The plural of RASOOL. The Messengers.

SA': Hour. Usually used to denote the Hour, that is the time when the world ends, and the YAWM AL AKHIRA begins.

SAA: A measure of volume, equal to four MUDDS.

SADAQA: Giving to the needy, in any form, including sharing wisdom, giving a helping hand, giving away clothing, food and money. SADAQA is given voluntarily in good will seeking only ALLAH's pleasure.

SAHIH: Healthy and sound with no defects.

SALAT: One of the pillars of ISLAM. It is the prayer which consists of fixed sets of standings, bowings, prostrations and sittings in worship to ALLAH. There are five prayers which are obligatory: SUBH which is done between dawn and sunrise; DHUR which is done between mid day and mid afternoon; 'ASR which is done between mid afternoon and sunset; MAGHRIB which is done immediately after sunset; and 'ISHA which is done between once it is dark and mid night. The MUSLIM day begins at MAGHRIB. It is necessary to be in GHUSL and in WUDU before you do the SALAT. SALAT is a purification outwardly and inwardly.

SALIH: A developed man. By definition, one who is in the right place at the right time.

SHAHADA: One of the pillars of ISLAM. It is to witness: "LA ILAHA IL'ALLAH, MUHAMMAD AR RASULU'LLAH" that is "There is no god only ALLAH, Muhammad is the Messenger of ALLAH," may the blessings and peace of Allah be on him. The SHAHADA is the gateway to ISLAM and the gateway to JINNAH. It is easy to say, but to act on it is a vast undertaking which has vast results, in both inward awareness and outward action. Affirming the SHAHADA is a purification outwardly and inwardly.

SHAHID: A witness, a martyr in the way of ALLAH.

SHARI'A: A road. The Way of Islam, the Way of Muhammad, may the blessings and peace of ALLAH be on him, the road which leads to knowledge of ALLAH and the Garden. Shaykh 'Abd al Qadir al Murabit writes, "It is the behaviour modality of a people based on the revelation of their Prophet. The last shari'a in history has proved to be that of Islam. Its social modality abrogates all previous shara'i e.g. Navaho, Judaic, Vedic, Buddhic, etc. These shara'i however, continue until the arrival and confrontation takes place in that culture with the final and thus superior shari'a – Islam. It is, being the last, therefore the easiest to follow, for it is applicable to the whole human race wherever they are." (Qur'anic Tawhid. Diwan Press. 1981).

SHAYTAN: A devil, particularly the Devil Iblis, may ALLAH curse him, who is one of the JINN who was and is too proud to obey ALLAH, and who encourages everyone else to be likewise. SHAYTAN is part of the creation of ALLAH, and we seek refuge in ALLAH from the evil that He has created.

SHIRK: To associate anything or anyone as a partner with ALLAH, that is, to worship what is other than ALLAH, including your self, your country, your universe and what it contains. SHIRK is the opposite of TAWHID. ALLAH says in QUR'AN that He will forgive any wrong action except SHIRK. Shaykh 'Abd al Qadir al Murabit writes, "Idol-worship means giving delineation to the Real. Encasing it in an object, a concept, a ritual, or a myth. This is called shirk, or association. Avoidance of shirk is the most radical element in the approach to understanding existence in Islam. It soars free of these deep social restrictions and so posits such a profoundly revolutionary approach to existence that it constitutes – and has done for fourteen hundred years – the most radical rejection of the political version of idolatory, statism. It is very difficult for programmed literates in this society to cut through to the clear tenets of Islam, for the Judaic and Christian perversions stand so strongly in the way either as, rightly, anathema, or else as ideals. The whole approach to understanding reality has a quite different texture than that known and defined in European languages, thus a deep insight into the structure of the Arabic language itself would prove a better introduction to the metaphysic than a philosophical statement. The uncompromising tawhid that is affirmed does not add on any sort of 'god-concept'. Nor does it posit an infra-god, a grund-god, even an over-god. Christian philosophers were so frightened by this position that when they met it, to stop people discovering the fantasy element in their trinitarian mythology they decided to identify it with pantheism in the hope of discrediting it. That they succeeeded in this deception is an indication of how far the whole viewpoint has been kept out of reach of the literate savage society. Let it suffice here to indicate that there is no 'problem' about the nature of Allah. Nor do we consider it possible even to speak of it. No how, who, or what or why. It is not hedging the matter in mystery. It is simply asking the wrong questions. The knowledge of Allah is specifically a personal quest in which the radical question that has to be asked is not even 'who am I?' but 'Where then are you going?' (Qur'anic Tawhid. Diwan Press. 1981).

SIDRAT AL MUNTAHA: The lote tree of the furthest limit. The place where form ends.

SIRAT AL MUSTAQIM: The straight path, of ISLAM.

SUNNA: The form, the customary practice of a person or group of people. It has come to refer almost exclusively to the practice of the Messenger of ALLAH, Muhammad, may the blessings and peace of Allah be on him, but at the time that Imam Malik, may ALLAH be pleased with him, compiled the Muwatta', there was no sense of setting the SUNNA of the Prophet apart from the SUNNA of Madina, so that the actions of its knowledgeable people were given even more weight than the behaviour of the Prophet related in isolated HADITH. The SUNNA of the prophet Muhammad and the first

MUSLIM community of MADINA AL MUNAWARRA is a complete behavioural science that has been systematically kept outside the learning framework of this society.

SURA: A form, a large unit of the QUR'AN linked by thematic content, composed of AYATS. Every SURA in QUR'AN has a particular form, and is named as such.

SURA AL FATIHA: The form of both Opening and Victory. This is the opening SURA of the QUR'AN. Recitation of SURA AL FATIHA is an integral and essential part of the SALAT, which means that every MUSLIM recites it at least twenty times a day. It is thus the most often daily repeated statement on the face of the earth today. Its translation in English is as follows:

In the Name of Allah, the Merciful, the Compassionate,

Praise to Allah, Lord of the worlds,
The Merciful, the Compassionate,
King of the Day of the Life-Transaction.
Only You we worship and only You we ask for help.
Lead us on the Straight Path,
The path of those whom you have blessed.
Not of those with whom you are angry, and not of those who are astray.

SURA YUNUS: The form of the prophet Jonah, on him be peace.

SURA YUSUF: The form of the prophet Joseph, on him be peace.

TAKBIR: The saying of "ALLAHU AKBAR", "ALLAH is Greatest". SALAT begins with TAKBIR.

TAQLID: In reference to FIQH, it means the following of previous authorities and the avoidance of IJTIHAD.

TAQWA: Awe of ALLAH, which inspires a person to be on guard against wrong action and eager for actions which please Him.

TASLIM: Giving the MUSLIM greeting of "AS SALAAMU 'ALAYKUM," "Peace be on you". SALAT ends with a TASLIM.

TASSAWUF: Sufism. Shaykh 'Abd al Qadir al Murabit writes, "Its preferred etymology is that it derives from suf, wool. Shaykh Hassan al-Basra said, "I saw forty of the people of Badr and they all wore wool." This means that the sufi – tasawwafa – has put on the wool. This is distinct from those who confirm the way of Islam with the tongue and by book learning. It is taking the ancient way, the primordial path of direct experience of the Real. Junayd said, "The sufi is like the earth, filth is flung on it but roses grow from it." He also said, "The sufi is like the earth which supports the innocent and the guilty, like the sky which shades everything, like the rain which washes everything." The sufi is universal. He has reduced and then eliminated the marks of selfhood to allow a clear view of the cosmic reality. He has rolled up the cosmos in its turn and obliterated it. He has gone beyond. The sufi has said 'Allah' – until he has understood. All men and women play in the world like children. The sufi's task is to recognise the end in the beginning, accept the beginning in the end, arrive at the unified view. When the outward opposites are the same, and the instant is presence, and the heart is serene, empty and full, light on light, the one in the woollen cloak has been robed with the robe of honour and is complete. The Imam also said, "If I had known of any science greater than sufism, I would have gone to it, even on my hands and knees."" (Qur'anic Tawhid. Diwan Press. 1981).

TAWBA: Turning away from wrong action to ALLAH and asking His Forgiveness. Returning to correct action after error. One of the greatest acts of TAWBA is to abandon the DEEN of KUFR and embrace the DEEN of ISLAM.

TAWHID: Unity in its most profound sense. ALLAH is One in His Essence and His

Attributes and His Acts. The whole universe and what it contains is One unified event which in itself has no reality. ALLAH is Real. Shaykh 'Abd al Qadir al Murabit writes, "Our Imam said, "It is a meaning which obliterates the outlines and joins the knowledges. Allah is as He always was. Tawhid has five pillars: it consists of the raising of the veil on the contingent, to attribute endlessness to Allah alone, to abandon friends, to leave one's country, and to forget what one knows and what one does not know." His greatest statement on tawhid, which Shaykh al-Akbar has called the highest of what may be said on the subject is, "The colour of the water is the colour of the glass." Commenting on this Shaykh Ibn 'Ajiba said, "This means that the exalted Essence is subtle, hidden and luminous. It appears in the outlines and the forms, it takes on their colours. Admit this and understand it if you do not taste it." Tawhid is itself a definition whose meaning is not complete for the one who holds to it until he has abandoned it or rather exhausted its indications and abandoned it for complete absorption in the One." (Qur'anic Tawhid. Diwan Press. 1981).

TAYAMMUM: Purification for prayer with clean dust, earth or stone, when water for GHUSL or WUDU is either unavailable or would be detrimental to health. TAYAMMUM is done by striking the earth with the palms of the hands and wiping the face and hands and forearms.

'ULAMA: The plural of 'Alim. MUSLIMS who have sound and complete outward knowledge manifested in action.

'UMRA: The lesser pilgrimage to the KA'ABA, the House of ALLAH in MAKKA, and the performance of its rites in the protected area which surrounds the KA'ABA. It can be done at any time of the year.

WAJIB: What is necessary, but not obligatory, in acts of worship in the SHARI'A.

WALI: The friend of ALLAH. The one who has both inward knowledge and outward knowledge. The station of the WALI is the station of knowledge of the Real by direct seeing. Inwardly the WALI has gnosis of ALLAH. He or she has intimate knowledge of the QUR'AN and HADITH, knowing their outward meanings and their inward meanings and their gnostic meanings, as much as ALLAH wills. Outwardly the WALI embodies the SHARI'A of ISLAM and the SUNNA of the prophet Muhammad, may the blessings and peace of Allah be on him. The greatest WALI, the QUTB, is like a drop compared to the ocean of the prophet Muhammad, may the blessings and peace of Allah be on him.

WUDU: Washing the hands, mouth, nostrils, face, forearms, head, ears, and feet, with water, in accordance with the SUNNA of the prophet Muhammad, may the blessings and peace of Allah be on him, so as to be pure for prayer. Once you have done WUDU, you remain in the state of WUDU until it broken by: any of the conditions which make it necessary to have a GHUSL; emission of impurities from the private parts – urine, faeces, wind, prostatic fluid, discharge; loss of consciousness by whatever means, usually by sleep or fainting; physical contact between man and woman where sexual pleasure is either intended or obtained; touching your penis with the inside of your hand or fingers; and leaving ISLAM. It is necessary to be in GHUSL and in WUDU to do the SALAT, and to hold the QUR'AN. WUDU is a purification both outwardly and inwardly.

YAQIN: Certainty. It has three stages;

> 'Ilm al yaqin, knowledge of certainty.
> 'Ayn al yaqin, source of certainty.
> Haqq al yaqin, truth of certainty.

The Raja of Mahmudabad defined them thus: You are told – there is a fire in the forest. You reach the fire in the forest and see it. You are the fire in the forest. (Qur'anic

Tawhid. Diwan Press. 1981).

YAWM AL AKHIRA: The Day After, the end of the world, and thus the Last Day, when everyone who has ever lived will be given life again, gathered together, their actions and intentions weighed in the Balance, and their place in either the Garden or the Fire confirmed. YAWM AL AKHIRA is also referred to in the QUR'AN as YAWM ID DEEN, the Day of the Life Transaction; YAWM AL BATH, the Day of Rising from the grave; YAWM AL HASHR, the Day of Gathering; YAWM AL QIYAMA, the Day of Standing; YAWM AL MIZAN, the Day of the Balance; and YAWM AL HISAB, the Day of Reckoning. That Day will either be the best day or the worst day of your life, depending on who you are and where you are going. The YAWM AL AKHIRA is accurately described in great detail in the QUR'AN and the HADITH.

ZAKAT: One of the Pillars of Islam. It is an annual tax paid only by MUSLIMS, and not the AHLU DHIMMA, on: accumulated wealth; merchandise; certain crops; certain live stock; and subterranean and mineral wealth. As soon as it is collected it is redistributed to those in need, as defined in QUR'AN. ZAKAT is a purification both outwardly and inwardly.

ZAKAT AL FITR: A small measure, one SAA, of a local staple food, usually grain or dried fruit, which is collected from, or on behalf of, every single MUSLIM in the community at the end of RAMADAN, and given to those in need, as defined in QUR'AN. ZAKAT AL FITR is a purification both outwardly and inwardly.

ZAMZAM: The well near the KA'ABA in MAKKA which provides the best water in the world.

Most of the definitions in this glossary are taken directly or derive from the books listed in the Bibliography, which should all be read in order to arrive at an understanding which is far beyond the scope of this book.

BIBLIOGRAPHY

QUR'AN from ALLAH. Translated by, inter alia, Muhammad Pickthall, and by Muhammad Yusuf Ali. Avoid gross mis translations by non muslims.

AL MUWATTA' of Imam Malik. Translated by 'A'isha 'Abdarahman at Tarjumana and Ya'qub Johnson. Diwan Press. 1982.

AL RISALA of Ibn Abi Zaid al Qairwani. Translated by Alh. Bello Muhammad Daura. Northern Nigerian Publishing Co. Ltd. 1983.

THE FOUNDATIONS OF ISLAM of Qadi 'Ayad. Translated by 'A'isha 'Abdarahman at Tarjumana. Diwan al Amir Publications. 1982.

THE SHIFA' of Qadi 'Ayad. Translated by 'A'isha 'Abdarahman at Tarjumana.

LIFE OF MUHAMMAD of Ibn Ishaq. Translated by Guillaume. Oxford University Press. 1978.

LIFE OF MUHAMMAD by Martin Lings. Allen and Unwin. 1983.

SAHIH OF IMAM BUKHARI. Translated by Dr. Muhammad Muhsin Khan. Crescent Publishing House. 1974.

SAHIH OF IMAM MUSLIM. Translated and published by Shri Muhammad Ashraf. 1976.

THE GARDENS OF THE RIGHTEOUS of Imam Nawawi. Translated by Zafrullah Khan.

MISHKAT AL MASABIH. Translated by Professor Robson. 1972.

FORTY HADITH of Imam Nawawi. Translated by Ezzedin Ibrahim and Denys Johnson-Davies. The Holy Qur'an Publishing House. 1976.

FORTY HADITH QUDSI from ALLAH. Translated by Ezzedin Ibrahim and Denys Johnson-Davies. The Holy Qur'an Publishing House. 1980.

KUFR by Shaykh 'Abd al Qadir al Murabit. Diwan Press. 1981.

ROOT ISLAMIC EDUCATION by Shaykh 'Abd al Qadir al Murabit. Diwan al Amir Publications. 1982.

SIGN OF THE SWORD by Shaykh 'Abd al Qadir al Murabit. Medina Press. 1984.

THE BOOK OF STRANGERS by Ian Dallas. Victor Gollancz. 1972.

THE WAY OF MUHAMMAD By Shaykh 'Abd al Qadir al Murabit. Diwan Press. 1974.

DIWANS OF THE DARQAWA. Translated by 'A'isha 'Abdarahman at Tarjumana. Diwan Press 1980.

THE DARQAWI WAY of Shaykh Mawlay al 'Arabi ad Darqawi. Translated by 'A'isha 'Abdarahman at Tarjumana. Diwan Press. 1979.

THE MEANING OF MAN by Shaykh 'Ali al Jamal. Translated by 'A'isha 'Abdarahman at Tarjumana. Diwan Press. 1978.

QUR'ANIC TAWHID by Shaykh 'Abd al Qadir al Murabit. Diwan Press. 1981.

JESUS, PROPHET OF ISLAM by Muhammad Ata'ur Rahim and Ahmad Thomson. Diwan Press. 1977.

A STUDY IN CHRISTIAN GENOCIDE by Muhammad Ata'ur Rahim and Ahmad Thomson.

THE BIBLE, THE QUR'AN AND SCIENCE by Maurice Bucaille. 1977.

THE GOSPEL OF BARNABAS. Translated by Laura and Lonsdale Ragg. Aisha Bawany Waqf. 1977.

THE PROTOCOLS OF THE ELDERS OF ZION.

THE THIRTEENTH TRIBE. A. Koestler. 1978.
Most of the books on EZRA POUND and the NUREMBERG TRIALS in the British Library.
AND many many others, here, there and everywhere.

The Prophet Muhammad said, may the blessings and peace of Allah be on him, that knowledge is the lost property of the mumin, so he may pick it up wherever he or she finds it.

Nothing is what it seems.
This book is for all those who are not satisfied with the official version, and who want the real thing.

There is no real thing, only the Real, ALLAH.

Dajjal

(The King who has no clothes) by Ahmad Thomson

At a time when many people are attempting to relate current events and trends in the world to interpretations of the prophecies contained in the Book of Revelations, and the writings of Nostrodamus, and the predictions of fashionable clairvoyants, the author has done much the same – but by referring specifically to some of the prophecies contained in the Qur'an and the recorded sayings of the Prophet Muhammad, may Allah bless him and grant him peace.

This book is not merely a catalogue of prophecies, since it does not concentrate so much on analysing specific events as on viewing life in general in twentieth century society. Nor is the book merely a 'religious' critique of an aimless society. Rather, it is a concise anthropological, historical, economical, sociological, psychological and spiritual comparative study of different kinds of society – for it examines and compares the outward existential behaviour, together with its inward psychological reality, not only of those who do not base their way of life on prophetic guidance, but also of those who do.

The author does not confine his assessment of life in the late twentieth century to this world alone, but also draws attention to what existed before it, and what awaits us beyond it, in order to arrive at a balanced perspective. In so doing, he indicates the nature of existence and of the self, and, more significantly, what it all means.